Magic, Religion
& Cannabis

Magic, Religion & Cannabis

Also by the author:

Hip Hop
Art After Midnight
Adventures in the Counterculture
The Octopus Conspiracy
True Ghost Stories
Cannabis Cures Cancer?
My Tragic Love Affair
Paradigms and Perceptions
My Chomsky Critique
The Bitcoin Revolution
The Ultimate Film Guide
Killing Lincoln: The Real Story
Dirty Money, Secret Societies and Killing JFK
1966
Hip Hop: The Complete Archives

Dedicated to James "Chef Ra" Wilson

How it all began

People often ask me how I turned into such an anti-establishment character and I explain it all happened in the 5th Grade.

I'd moved around a lot, from Boston to Cambridge, England, to Munich, Germany, back to central Illinois, where I was born. So when I entered 4th Grade at Yankee Ridge I was bilingual and spoke German with a perfect Bavarian accent.

It was hard making friends with all those changes. But it got even harder the next year because I was moved to Leal School when my Dad bought a Tudor-style brick house on Delaware Street. Leal was very different from upscale Yankee Ridge, much more working-class. Phillip Patton (sitting next to me in the center of the front row) had a little gang he started with three or four of his buddies. I sat behind Phil and he tried to recruit me. *West Side Story* had recently come to the Princess Theater and that movie deeply affected me. I understood instinctively that forming a gang was a noble quest, but instead of joining up with Phil, I decided to create my own. Andy Miller (top row, second from right) was my initial co-conspirator in this mission, and all the early meetings were held at his house. I must have pulled the rest from another class. There were about six of us to start. I do remember Eric Steffenson (who would die tragically young) was one of us.

For some bizarre reason, I named us "The Roaring 21 Club" and we had a secret sign, which was a perpendicular line with two horizontal bars. Maybe it was a takeoff on a Christian cross since I was still a Lutheran at the time, attending Sunday school every week.

When a big snowfall hit town, I challenged Phil and his gang to a snowball fight in Carle Park. Unbeknownst to Phil, however, right after he accepted this challenge, I went around school recruiting about 30 extra members for my group, most of which came from lower classes. I quickly gathered them all in the pavilion on the east side of the park and taught them the secret sign so they would be official members. Bugsy was one of my initiates at that point.

At the appointed hour, Andy and I stood in the center of the park with three or four others, while the rest hid in the bushes around the perimeter. Before long, Phil and his gang came screaming into the park with gobs of snowballs in their arms. When they got close, however, I gave the signal and everybody came running in, surrounding them, pelting them with snowballs. They valiantly tried to make a fight of it, forming a circle with their backs together, but it quickly evolved into a remake of Custer's Last Stand, so they took off running towards Dennis Seth's house, which was their nearest refuge. We followed, raining snowballs on their backs. When we got to the house, we pelted it with snowballs. There was a jar of nails on the porch that got broken. As soon as that happened, I pulled my troops back to the park and boy, did we have a hearty chuckle, many of us bent over double, others writhing on the ground, as I recounted the engagement from the battlefield, pointing out where the various highlights had taken place. "Did you see the look on Phil's face when he realized the was surrounded?!! Hahahaa!"

But the next day, Phil got called into the principal's office over something he'd done, and while there, he told the story of the snowball fight. The principal wanted to see everyone involved and when we showed up, he had to move the meeting from his office to the gym. He lined up Phil's gang on one side, and mine on the other; it was like 40 versus five. He looked at me and said, "Do you consider this a fair fight?"

I didn't know what to say. It was just a snowball fight, fer christsake, I'm thinking. But that principal made sure when I moved to junior high I was put in a program for problem kids. My classes were weird, full of people with learning disabilities and serious issues with violence. It wasn't until I got to high school that I realized other classes weren't like mine. Other classes actually had serious discussions and were learning all sorts of stuff, while I was basically being warehoused in a room filled with dangerous bullies and idiots. I blame it all on *West Side Story*. Phil later confronted me in the schoolyard and we had a fistfight to settle things that became quite a famous showdown at the school, gathering a crowd that was evenly split between who they wanted to root for. Phil boxed me in the ear pretty hard. It was my first fight so I just landed body blows. I didn't have the guts to swing for the face or head, not yet, anyway.

When I look back on this now, I realize the creation of secret societies is probably wired into our DNA. Another thing that springs to mind: Within a few years The Merry Pranksters would become my biggest role models, accomplished scouts of the fun vibe, who replaced my media-induced street-gang mythology with

The Magic Bus, the real secrets of which remain little-known today. I know a few. Not as much as Babbs, Mountain Girl, Wavy or Krassner, and the grandmaster now resides in the unknown dimensions, but this I do know: The snowball fight was a prank. Nobody got hurt. Under Prankster rules, I should not have been shamed, and my education should not have been torpedoed. How many kids in America were there like me, shunted into a separate education system for lost causes and instigators?

Reading Red Cloud

To be honest, this was my first and only attempt at a mushroom tea ceremony, but it was epic, although briefly scary. My advice after 50 years of experimentation is: avoid all synthetics and pills. Peyote is my favorite psychedelic, although cannabis is the only one safe for daily use.

My first psychedelic peace pole was planted in the Florida Keys. I recommend planting these to collect and amplify peaceful vibrations. The more effort you put into painting, carving, and decorating these poles, the more magic they will produce. And the same goes for peaceful ceremonies held around them: The vibrations resonant long after the ceremony is over.

The author during a jam session with Plunker,
who performs with a handmade two-string guitar.

By the time I went to my first National Rainbow
Gathering, I'd already been hanging out with Garrick Beck in the
East Village for over a year, and also attending the Rainbow
picnics in Central Park, which I stumbled onto by accident one
afternoon. I remember being stunned to find Julian Beck and
Judith Malina living around the corner from me on West End
Avenue when I moved into a $120 a month room on the Upper
West Side in 1979.

Later, I'd meet their son Garrick when I joined the garage band
scene of the Lower East Side. So when I arrived at my first
gathering, I came well prepared and carried water-based florescent
paints so I could make signs, paint faces and customize my camp.
I built an elaborate complex right below Garrick. I remember one
Rainbow moved out of the area complaining about the "condos"
moving in. Truth is, every bit of dead wood I formed into
couches, floors and structures, ended up burnt in Fantuzzi's giant
fire-pit, and boy was he happy to have all those pre-cut logs. I'd
never met Fantuzzi, but quickly figured out he was important
when the midnight jam sessions started going off with him as the

star attraction. Tuzzi had walked in and done the same thing as me: "Where's Garrick?" And then pitched his tent as close as possible. Plunker was there too, and Kid Village and Felipe were next door.

My cousins had access to one of the few undeveloped parts of the Florida Keys.

Of course, my life turned 180 degrees after that experience. I'd been focused on the garage band scene at the time and leading my band the Soul Assassins to rock'n'roll glory on the Hemp Tour, but suddenly I had an urge to put a major effort into spreading the Rainbow Peace Vibe. First thing I wanted to do was visit my cousins in Florida to enlist them into the mission. Tom had saved me in 1970 by buying a one-way ticket to Stockholm so I could escape the Vietnam War, an experience both my cousins had been through and neither wanted me anywhere close to that national nightmare. Now it was time for me to pay him back.

After Vietnam, my cousins had spent a few years traveling around the world. I maintained correspondence with them during this time, and kept everything, including all the Vietnam letters. Someday I'll publish those letters, as Tom is a great writer and very funny. He had one dangerous incident, when he was attacked while hiking in the Himalaya's. Both my cousins became anti-war activists after leaving the army. Eventually, they settled in Delray Beach and got jobs as lifeguards, but they had a secret hideout in the Florida Keys, where they would go on vacations whenever they had time off. I went there to initiate them. My plan was to build a private gathering, something that might convince both my cousins to join me at an upcoming regional in Ocala, Florida, where I would be camping with the Freedom Fighters.

I painted signs and decorations everywhere with non-toxic paint.

Before my cousins arrived I constructed a giant peace pole and designed some ceremonial spaces. There were psychedelic signs everywhere. I had a bag of mushrooms and brewed up some mushroom tea, the drinking of which would be our first ritual.

Reading from Red Cloud during the tea ceremony.

Just to get the right vibe going, after the mushroom tea and ceremonial face painting, I started reading from the autobiography of Red Cloud. Most people don't realize the counterculture came out of Congo Square in New Orleans, and it started as a merger between Black African slaves who had been living in Haiti working the sugar plantations and the local native Americans. You can see the Native influence in the New Orleans ceremonies of today. That influence is huge on hippie culture as well, and it's a path for all people to experience vibes of Native culture without actually becoming a wannabe because our version is a hybrid of all cultures, which is what Rainbow is really all about. After an OM around the Peace Pole and some drumming and chanting, it was time to get into the boats. My cousins had two sailboats at the time, a big one and a little one.

Jerry built the little one himself, as well as the trailer he lugged it around with. It was a masterful craft, very fast and seaworthy. As I recall, there was a race to see which boat would get launched first and Jerry won easily. Once we were out near the Gulfstream, it was time to go snorkeling, one of our favorite things to do in the Keys, and this was before the pollution killed most of the coral.

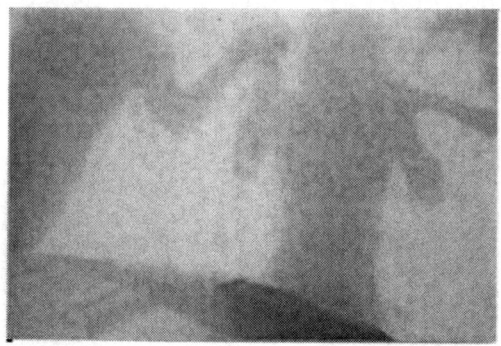

The underwater 4:20 OM was a spontaneous event,
but I made sure it was documented.

Then I got the inspiration to do an underwater 4:20 OM, which actually worked out fantastic since we could all hear each other clearly and it seemed to have a calming effect on the ocean around us.

After the underwater OM, I got fascinated by a lonely baby jellyfish and followed the transparent little creature back to his nest, where thousands of relatives were breathing in unison. I was

17

thinking about doing an OM with them, but then suddenly snapped out of my mushroom fog and realized what a dangerous situation I was in. Very suddenly I was swimming full-speed back to the boat.

We loaded up on the big boat and headed back to the safety of our camp. It was a great week, and I had a blast creating my little hippie Disneyland, but, in truth, although my cousins went along and joined in on the ceremonies, they didn't get drawn in enough to want to ever attend a Rainbow Gathering, which had been my major motivation for creating the entire spectacle in the first place. In fact, Jerry admitted he'd accidentally stumbled into the Ocala Gathering one year and been scared off and freaked out by the sight of naked hippies. That was the difference between us. I'd joined the counterculture as a teen just while they'd joined the army, so hippie gatherings for me was like home. Why it's so hard for some to get over the nakedness I'll never know. It's just another form of freedom, and if you never use it, you aren't really free.

The Fun Vibe

There are a lot of vibe trails, good and bad, but the fun vibe is the best. It's a delicate trail, easily lost. Sometimes it can disappear for decades. As legend goes, Neal Cassady surfed the hum of a gearshift, scouted the fun vibe and gave it to the Beat Crew. The Pranksters got the trail from Cassady and shared it with Jerry Garcia, Timothy Leary and the Beatles. Some people dream about being a rock star, but I always dreamed of being a Merry Prankster and riding Furthur's top deck with Cassady at the helm.

In 1997, High Times began advertising the first Hemp World's Fair in Oregon, just a few miles from where Ken Kesey, Ken Babbs and the Merry Pranksters were living. My hope was to combine forces with the best vibe scouts I knew, and hold a ceremony to tune into the sacred fun vibe.

Early in the spring, I flew out to Oregon and met Ken Babbs and the owner of a possible 15-acre site, a mercurial fellow named Bill Conde. Well, the site looked good and plans were going great. The focal point of the event was going to be a silent meditation on Sunday, from dawn until noon, followed by an OM. Babbs gave the event its name (Whee!). But we hit a glitch as the Pranksters unexpectedly pulled out just two weeks into preparations.

"We have to do a July tour in Europe for our record company," said Babbs sadly over the phone. But we still had Stephen Gaskin, Paul Krassner, John Trudell, Dennis Peron and a bunch of other good vibe scouts. It was too late to call Whee! off. Something I've learned that hard way over the years, the bigger the ceremony the more delicate the negotiations. I'd also secured a date right after the Rainbow National Gathering, which was happening close nearby, which guaranteed a huge turnout, although most of them would end up volunteering and working on the crew.

After a few months of preparation, I arrived to start construction. Although the main stage was built and water and power lines had

21

been dug for some booths and kitchens, it was really just a barren field with a two-story pile of twisted metal, rotten wood and garbage piled in the center. About 40 people were camped around the property. Six22, Zero and Roberto rode into camp with me.

Just looking at the pile of garbage made me dizzy. The Oregon sun was blazing. The only shade was a grove of pine trees way over in the parking lot. I knew the crew would melt down quick unless they got a steady supply of food and water. Fortunately, Sun Dog Kitchen was on site, straight from the nearby Rainbow Gathering. I entered Sun Dog camp and immediately caught sight of some freshly born pups.

"Aww, puppies," I said lurching forward to pet them.

Like a fearless Zen master, the mom darted out from under a picnic table and sunk two teeth into my Levis at the knee.

"Damn," I said, "You just ruined by best rainbow-stripe jeans." Meanwhile, I'm thinking what a bad omen this is. After I customize my jeans, I tend to get overly attached to them.

I fingered the hole and noticed the strike was surgical, not a mark on my flesh. The Sun Dog crew jumped out of the corners to get between me and the angry mom.

"There's no dogs….supposed to be here," I snarled.

Roberto appeared. "I have a dog," he said wistfully. "Look, there's dogs all over the place." As he swept his hand across the horizon, I noticed three or four more dogs scampering about.

Lee, Stevie D's straw boss, let me know he was vexed by the mission of preparing 3,000 free meals over the next week.

"Whatta ya need, Lee?" I said. "Give me a wish list."

I walked out into the field and called council. Mostly young brothers came, many of whom seemed to be from One love Zion Train, a tour group sponsored by Universal Life Church of One Love. They handed me an envelop filled with flyers and propaganda on their noble quest to scout the vibe all summer.

"Come on, boys," I shouted. "We're on a sacred mission to build hippie Disneyland! And we only got six days to do it!"

"What do you want us to do?" asked five voices and 40 faces.

"First, we gotta get rid of that pile of trash!"

In a matter of seconds, 80 hands hit the garbage pile and began separating it out for disposal at the local recycling center.

"Come on Stoney," I said walking toward the rented Ford pickup. "We gotta make a supply run. Where's that wish list?"

Before the day was through, Stoney and I visited every discount center in Eugene, and that Ford was filled with enough food and drink for 50 people for three days, along with every other type of supplies we might need, including 20 pairs of work gloves and a precious erase board and five fluorescent markers.

At sundown, after we made it back to the site, the garbage pile was half gone. A gorgeous sunset cloud formation appeared over the stage, while behind me, an almost full moon rose over the mountains. A dozen geese flew past in V formation. "Squawk, squawk," said Alpha Goose as they whooshed toward the sunset. I felt a blast of bird energy and knew they were scouting their vibe trail. Sun Dog blew the conch for dinner. We circled up, held hands and did an OM, followed by everyone throwing their hands in the air and yelling, "Whee!!!"

July 14, 1997

"We believe in doing what is right and respecting others, with no judgments or dogma, only true love and respect for all living beings," read the flyer from the Zion Crew. "All faiths are connected to the One and the One is connected to us. The train is an ongoing experience for the caravaners of voluntarily spreading the unity love vibrations that make this the 30th anniversary of the Summer of Love."

I was sitting in the back of an RV parked next to the stage, where we'd set up Mission Control. The radios arrived late, so it was hard to get the crews properly coordinated. So far, we had 14 members of Sun Dog and 73 other assorted volunteers on site.

Garrick Beck rolled in, set up his tipi and split. Garrick, Plunker and John Buffalo were crew chiefs on the Temple Dragon Crew (TDC), which was supposed to handle people problems inside the venue and protect the ceremonial spaces.

Hippie security is a little-known art form that has been evolving inside the counterculture for 50 years. Groups like the Diggers in Haight-Ashbury were among the earliest proponents of this art form. Whenever anything bad would happen on the streets of the Haight, local residents could be depended upon to handle the problem using only nonviolent persuasion. For example, if some brother disrespected a sister, that person would suddenly find themselves surrounded by people wanting to discuss, in a quiet, rational manner, why the brother felt it was okay to be disrespectful. The fact no one would resort to anger or violence would usually throw the perpetrator so off-guard that he'd end up analyzing and apologizing for his inappropriate behavior. Techniques of nonviolent communication were eventually perfected even more by the Merry Pranksters, who knew hos to "create a movie," pull a person into that movie and alter the perceptual frame of reference of a situation to their own benefit.

Many professional security guards and police rely on telepathic hostility and thinly veiled threats of physical harm to enforce rules. But hippie security never resorts to hints of violence. Every security situation is unique and negotiable. Over the past 40 years, the Rainbow Family Gathering has been a superb training ground for people interested in studying nonviolent security techniques. The Shanti Sena (peace eyes) is the name that has evolved for this group.

Fortunately, Amazin' Dave, one of the best of the Rainbow Shanti Sena, showed up, and I hired him on the spot. He moved into the Mission Control RV with me to handle the late-night problems. Six22 was handling all medical problems His cat Ganja moved into the RV with me and Dave. By the end of the day, the garbage pile was gone and the fence was ready to go up.

July 16

The professional, licensed-and-bonded company we hired for 24-hour security had rolled in and set up on the 15th. I explained we had our own internal security crew and I wanted them to work the perimeter and guard the fence, but I didn't want them to deal with people inside. That job was for the TDC. If we had something we couldn't handle, we would call in the professional security. I had little faith in these professional, however, as it appeared to be a couple of biker types supported by two black teenagers, one of who had to be told to stop setting off firecrackers as brush fire was one of our biggest issues. The lead biker dude made a point of making fun of my hat in front of me, and obviously had authority issues.

However, during the night, these professionals suddenly packed up and left without any explanation. I stayed up all night at the front gate without a single other guard on duty, feeling like Michael Corleone at the hospital, and wondering if the professionals weren't called away in preparation for some swat-team raid on the event.

I'd sent word to Garrick and Plunker that whoever showed up first would be "put in charge." This was my bait to draw them quickly out of the gathering, something they were loath to do as they worked on cleanup most years back then. This tactic backfired though because John Buffalo arrived first, so I anointed him the Chief of the Temple Dragons. You can't believe what a problem this created with Plunker, who immediately felt insulted when he heard that news.

Meanwhile, Diego's bus rolled in to setup the Gypsy Village, and Felipe's bus rolled in to setup Family Village. The site map had changed drastically already, so I drew the current map on the erase board and discussed possible locations. Both crews picked new sites and started putting up tents and tarps. The Gypsies brought a huge circus tent for workshops and seminars. We had a fence crew, sign painting crew, vendor staking crew, carpenter crew, fire pit crew, kitchen crew, Gypsy crew, tipi circle crew, stage crew and Family Village crew all working feverishly by mid-afternoon.

The biggest change in the map came when I staked a huge area overlooking a small pond as Doggie Village. There were supposed to be about 50 vendors on that very spot, and I was already wondering how I was going to explain this to people who had paid for those booths.

July 17

The vendors started arriving early in the day, and most were shocked to find the site map wasn't the same anymore. Beth, who had been recently hired as vending director of the Hemp Expo, was greeting vendors as they rolled in. Poor Beth was engulfed by hysteria. I could identify with her situation and tried to help. The most remarkable thing about the event was the way Beth kept her head together and never melted down once.

Most of the vendors were actually quite nice and friendly and easy to deal with once the new site was explained. However, we had a few problem cases, like the Babylon vendor, who was selling Pepsi and toxic hot dogs out of an RV with a generator. I put him in Bus Village, where he belonged. He happily took the spot, but by the end of the day, he tore down the fence separating Bus Village from the site and demanded to be moved inside. Garrick moved him to the Gypsy camp, but the Gypsy crew exploded after he turned on his generator. The fumes were blowing right into the Casbah Tea House. So we moved him again, this time right next to our beautiful first pit, where his exhaust blew into the amphitheater. Even so, he kept complaining about all the money he was losing.

"Nobody wants your Babylon food," I said finally. "Why don't you go solar and sell organic food, or better yet, pack up and leave?" Of course, he was making plenty of money and had no intention of leaving.

Around this time, most of the High Times staff were arriving for the first time, and there was tremendous confusion between Bill Conde, who I suspected was a tweaker from his mood swings, the Rainbows and Temple Dragons, and the newly arriving High Times staff. Once we had 10,000 people on site, the event took on a telepathic energy all its own, and there was quite a power struggle going on, and lots of shouting over the radios. Meanwhile, some of the High Times staff were going around asking the crew why they took orders from me considering they weren't being paid. They wanted to know what I was doing wrong, so they could do their job, which I guess was to keep me in line and under control.

Meanwhile, Plunker was calling his own secret councils and had the real center of energy on security at the event. He must have personally brought a hundred Shanti Sena onto the Dragon crew, and he also let most of them know he wasn't getting the proper respect from me because Buffalo had been anointed Chief of Security. I was oblivious to ego struggles at the time, and it took many years for me to sort out some of the scenarios that went down at the event, so complex were the energies involved. When I saw *Saving Private Ryan*, it reminded me a lot of staging hippie festivals.

I'd had major issues with Conde's lawyer, who tried to engineer himself into a paid position as one of the Temple Dragon chiefs, which I thought was a conflict of interest, taking money from me and Conde. The one job that lawyer had been assigned was hiring the medical crew, and he'd told me months earlier that wasn't a problem and he had it under control, but after I told him "no salary " he dropped that ball, and the day before the event was scheduled to open, he threatened me with a lawsuit because I had no medical team in place, which was a provision of the contract. I never felt so sucker-punched in my life and I began melting down with anger.

Plunker came to the rescue and led an OM circle in the RV, calming my rage down to manageable levels. After that Plunker stopped acting hostile and decided to put his crew to work building a proper fire pit. Fire was a real hazard, due to a lot of dry straw on the ground and Plunker is the best firefighter I know, having served under him during the Great Wyoming Fire, when several thousand Rainbows stomped out a three-acre blaze that topped the trees and threatened to destroy an entire national forest.

The fire pit was heart-shaped, facing the Gypsy stage, with four rows of amphitheater seating carved out of a mound of earth displaced to make the pit. It was so beautifully constructed I almost burst into tears just looking at it. Felipe cam down from Family Village to sanctify us with sage and prayer as we lit the ceremonial flame at 4:20 PM.

That night, the vendor crew stayed up until 3 AM leading convoys of vendors into the site, making sure their vehicles were parked safely and didn't block the fire roads.

July 18

On opening day, midwife Daphne Singingtree and her event medical team arrived to take charge of the medical movie. Daphne had been lobbying me hard for the job three months earlier, so I was happy to see she got her wish. Meanwhile, some of the crew members remained in "frantic mode" and didn't pick up on the cool Temple Dragon style. These unfortunates were easy to identify by the big knots of tension on their third eyes, and the fact they circled endlessly around some imaginary issue, unable to move forward or make a clear decision. I sometimes two such characters in my face at the same time and no logic worked on their minds. I'd already lost my voice from inhaling dust and cannabis smoke, plus trying to talk to a crew of 100 people throughout the day and night for days. Once the event started, I tried to remain as quiet and low-key as possible.

"Listen," I told one of the High Times crew softly. "I've got an important mission for you. I want you to do to Sun Dog, pour yourself some fresh lemonade and wait until I get there."

Peter Gorman was one of High Times crew who instantly integrated into the movie, so I put him in charge of Mission Control and started calling him Commander Gorman. Early in the day, some of the Shanti Sena had called in supply requests over the radio that Peter didn't feel like dealing with that moment as he was also running the stage. In retaliation, some Dragons changed the name of his post to Mission Impossible and that tag stuck for the remainder of the event.

The parking lots were in chaos. Conde had demanded control of parking because he wanted all the parking fees for himself, but when I suggested parking was crucial and we ought to put Garrick or Plunker in charge of that operation, Conde and his lawyer ridiculed me, saying they had much more important issues to deal with than working the parking lot.

But only a few hours into the event, the roads became hopelessly clogged and our main parking lot useless because vehicles had been allowed to enter and park willy-nilly. A lot that should have held another hundred vehicles was impassable, and the grand entrance I'd designed for our venue worthless, so clogged with vehicles that no one could get close to the front gate.

Even thought the roads and parking were in chaos, inside the venue was peaceful hippie heaven, with lots of good food at low prices. The stage was even running close to the printed schedule. The 420 Show with the Cannabis Cup Band rocked and was the main event of the day. We had New York City's best sound engineer Charlie Martin working the board.

A dinner council I could barely talk above a whisper, so I asked Garrick to crew chief the council. I drew a map of the erase board to show all the latest changes and where the new fire lanes were. That's when all hell broke loose. Everyone was pissed about the problems in the parking lot, as well as the lack of laminates for free food. For about an hour there was a lot of hot air, but no solutions. Then Gideon spoke. Gideon is not the sort of brother who does a lot of talking at council. Although he's a big bear of a man, he scouts a very mellow vibe. But Gideon was all fired up, like Crazy Horse talking to the Lakota warriors before the Custer fight. He laid down a plan to get a new parking lot across the street and put traffic coordinators to monitor the flow. He volunteered to hold down that job all night if necessary. Then he led the crew in a chant of "break even, break even." I was especially happy Gideon had put some perspective on the issue, because I knew some of the volunteers were grumbling about the huge numbers of people and how much money High Times must be making, not realizing it's nearly impossible to break even on a first time event.

July 19

I drove into camp around 8 AM, having spent the night at the Ramada Inn. Gideon was still on the front gate, a big wad of cash in his fanny pack. I parked and walked around camp, moving signs to their proper locations, stocking the info booth with schedules, and checking to make sure the fire lanes behind the booths were clear. While I walked my TDC patrol on the backline, I pulled up on a huge spotted male dog, who could have been cast as White Fang in a Jack London movie. The dog held my stare for a long time, and I continued to stare as I reached for my radio.

"Mission Impossible, we got a big alpha off his leash."

"This is Doggie Village, what's your twenty?"

"Between Doggie Village and Gypsy tent."

"We'll pick up the dog."

31

"Ten-four, over and out."

It was amazing how fast the radio could fix things. It was like a magic wand that made energy clouds appear like so many snow devils. Later that day, I got a big surprise when Ken Kesey, Ken Babbs and Mountain Girl, plus assorted other Pranksters, all wearing green masks, pulled up in front of Mission Impossible in a white Cadillac convertible. Babbs jumped out of the back seat and showed me his watch.

"Look," he said triumphantly, "it's exactly 4:20!"

"Commander Gorman, get this crew on stage immediately!" I shouted.

"Ten-four," said Peter.

Babbs handed me a green hemp scarf with rainbow stripes. It had two holes cut for my eyes. There was a lot of noise and telepathic chaos, what with the arrival of so many grandmasters of the vibe at once. Everyone was pressing toward us because they wanted to meet the famous Pranksters. But I had a private telepathic moment with Babbs, when time slowed and the background faded. He spoke to me in a silent way only Kenmasters know how to do.

"If you put on my magic mask," he said, "you'll become invisible."

A flock of geese flew overhead, maybe the same flock as before. Suddenly everything sped up and got crazy again and next thing I knew I was on stage wearing the mask, being introduced by Fantuzzi as Phoenix 420.

"One week ago, I fell asleep in the back of a car after a party," I said. "When I woke up, the car was parked in the center of this field. Only it didn't look like this. There was no hippie

32

Disneyland. There was only a two-story pile of twisted metal, wood and garbage. And forty hungry, homeless hippies. And we built this New Jerusalem! I guess they wanted me to say this because I was one of the crew that worked so hard. So let's hear it for the crew, especially the volunteers. In case you don't know, Whee's name came from Ken Babbs. He's one of the Merry Pranksters, the greatest fun vibe scouts of our time. The Merry Pranksters couldn't be here because of some Babylonian record-company tour. But we do have the Green Vipers, so let's a have a warm welcome for the Green Vipers!"

Kesey had already taken the stage as he obviously felt my introduction was overly long. Meanwhile, I melted into the crowd to explore my newfound invisibility, while the Pranksters launched into a song about a speed freak, which I thought appropriate considering Bill Conde's hyper mood changes. I could hear Bill screaming from the audience when I mentioned the big pile of garbage the crew had cleared. "What garbage??!!"

Just then the strangest thing happened. I began reading auras for the first time in my life. The overwhelming majority of people at the event were radiating happy vibrations. But there was a very small minority with darker emanations, a list that included Bill Condi. Instead of walking around the site, I found myself seated on the ground in a hidden spot with a clear view of the kids' playground we'd erected. I was convinced an evil force was mingling with the kids, and I began playing close attention to a tall, middle-aged man with a military haircut who was hanging out at the vending booth next to the playground. He was watching the kids play on the homemade swings and jungle gym. I noticed this man did not have a wristband, indicating he had not paid to enter the venue. I decided to work a Temple Dragon movie on him, so I walked up with a big smile on my face.

"Howdy, brother. Having fun yet?"

He eyed me suspiciously and gave no comment.

"Hey, where's your wristband?" I continued. "Everybody's got to have a wristband."

He smirked but said nothing.

"I've got some extra wristbands if you need one," I continued, reaching into my purple hemp fanny pack. "You should put one on so security doesn't kick you out. If you can't afford to pay the admission fee, that's no problem, I'll give you a wristband anyway. But if you can make a donation, we'd really appreciate it because it we didn't break even on this event yet. In fact, looks we're going to lose money. So if you could afford a small donation for the wristband, we'd really appreciate it."

"I don't *haf* any money," he said with a thick German accent.

"No problem," I said putting the band on his wrist. "Why not just open your wallet and show me? And if it's empty, then you don't have to pay anything."

There was a long pause and I watched him take mental notes on my Temple Dragon belt, with its radio, flashlight, medical supplies and various Batman-like emergency tools. He knew he was dealing with someone who could call in reinforcements. Although I was all smiles and happiness on the outside, inside I was beaming telepathic messages that I knew what he was all about and I could read his mind like a book. Rather than show me his wallet, he reached in his pocket, pulled out a wad of cash and handed me a twenty.

"Gee, thanks," I said.

Just then Plunker and Felipe walked by and I made a big deal of introducing them to the stranger. But he abruptly broke off from us and walked away without telling us his name.

"There something funny about him," I said. "He's been staring at the kids and I don't like his vibes."

Plunker and Felipe nodded their heads and agreed he seemed a bit out of place at the event. We began spreading word among the other TDC to keep an eye on him. But he must have realized something was up because he left the site within an hour and never came back.

July 20

By 8 AM, it was apparent Sunday was going to go into the high 90s with high humidity. A silent meditation was planned for the main meadow. We made a supply run for ice, water, soda and coolers. As we passed Family Village, the "no smoking of any kind" zone, Felipe the ceremony crew chief emerged.

"We better postpone the ceremony until sundown," I said. "Otherwise people will be fainting out there. We also need a pole for people to circle around."

"I'll work on that," said Felipe.

On the way back to Mission Impossible, I changed the daily event sign at the entrance to read: "OM at sunset."

I rode the TDC trail for the rest of the day, cruising in Gideon's golf cart. "This is more fun than golfing," I told everyone. I found two kids at Family Village who wanted to see if their mom was at Doggie Village. "Wanna go for a ride? Only if Felipe says okay."

I took the back fire lane so they had a great view of the pond on one side and the dog run on the other. All sorts of dogs came out to greet us as we cruised past, some staked and some running free. When we got to the corner, I noticed White Fang all fenced in by himself in Doggie Jail.

"Why is that doggie in jail?"

"Because he's not a nice doggie."

"Can we go inside Doggie Village now?"

"Yes, here's your mommy."

As I drove off, I heard the kids shouting, "Mommy there's been a mistake! This is not a bad doggie!"

The kids tore open the door to the jail and the Doggie Village crew came running.

"Mission Impossible, we got a jailbreak at Doggie Village. Two dangerous suspects from Family Village, about four feet high, just tore down the walls of Doggie Jail."

But White Fang walked out so meek and gentle and grateful to those kids, that the Doggie Village crew never put him back into Doggie Jail again. Isn't it funny how adults can learn from kids?

Mission Impossible called me on the radio to tell me the Krishna crew wanted to come into camp for free. I drove to the gate to greet them and make sure they were comfortable. "Be sure and catch the OM at sunset," I told them.

Backstage, there was the typical moment of confusion because I always insist the ceremonies be as spontaneous as possible, with lots of improvisation and no script. Naturally, this drives the tech-

36

heads and most of the High Times crew up a wall! And the ceremony crew gets blamed for ruining the clockwork precision of their rock show.

But because it was Sunday, the stage manager Alvin gladly powered up the wireless so Felipe could scout the vibe by the sacred peace pole that had been hastily erected. An old, well-traveled pole it was, with lots of carvings and a purple quartz crystal on top. Gaskin, Plunker, Garrick and many others started to form a circle around the pole, but the circle got confused because there were too many people for just one circle in such a small space.

A Japanese monk jumped on the line and began spiraling it toward the center. Everyone got involved in the spiral hand-dance. When it ended, everyone was holding hands. A call went out for the crew to come to the pole. Gaskin and I walked slowly to the pole and were actually the first to touch it. I gave it a hug, while the entire 300-person crew hugged me. Tear ducts burst open in every eye, and moved around the circle like a wave in a stadium. My heart was fully opened, and I sobbed with joy.

Then came the Whee! OM.

"We cranked the vibe," I said hugging Gaskin.

July 22

Babbs came out to the Ramada to meet the cleanup crew. Six22, Zero, Tammy, Donna Eagle, Alvin, Edison, G. Moses and me. We held a playful ceremony upon his arrival and Babbs was so honored he made up a song on the spot just for our pleasure.

When is all right to be too tight?
I can think of one extraordinary night when it was all right to be too tight.

37

I was so drunk I couldn't even stand up.
I fell asleep on the riverbank.
The cops came and arrested everybody else and they never got
me.
So it was all right to be too tight.
But you still....can't....roll....the joints....too tight.

"Thank you, thank you," said Babbs. "That was a spontaneous song I've been practicing for the last twenty-two years and this was the first I've had a chance to sing it. I want to thank you for lasting through the whole thing."

After the song, I filled Babbs in on the baby girl that had been born in the pine trees at 2:22 Monday morning.

"There was a cry in the woods of 'help me, help me,' and TDC came running fast because we thought a sister was being raped. Her cousin was with her and said, 'Calm down, everybody, Jamie's just having a baby.' The cousin caught the baby coming out, and was assisted by a former EMT medic named Sunray. The baby was named Cassady Sunflower Phoenix. The cord was tied with Amazin' Dave's hemp twine. Garrick and Six22 were on the scene. I rolled up just as the baby popped out and interviewed everyone involved. Daphne Singingtree was there, too. It was a real warrior birth. That child might be a great leader some day."

"It just goes to show to go that when things happen, they come into a lot of minds at the same time," said Babbs.

Babbs wanted drink, but the crew kept feeding him water and pizza. "Don't end up like Jack," I said. "Don't melt down and stay melted. *Big Sur*, that was his best book. He could've called it *Big Meltdown*."

"Kerouac, Ginsberg, they died relatively young," said Babbs. "It'd be great if they were still around. Cassady was unique. All the factions of the Beat crew revolved around Cassady because he knew what they were all talking about. They all strove to be like Cassady. You know what it was? Cassady really dealt on the lag. The one-thirtieth of a second between when you think of something and when you say it. He was always trying to beat the lag. So what he said had to do with what was happening right then. That was Cassady's thing. And he was always working on it as an artist. And at a certain point he knew that's what he was doing. But it was such a dangerous thing because speed freaks would try to emulate him, to be rapping all the time, but they weren't talking about anything, whereas Cassady was really talking about something. He was the true Avataar. The True Seeker of the Vibe."

Then the crew introduced Babbs to Cassady the dog, the same dog the kids had busted out of Doggie Jail.

"He was abandoned on the site," said Six22. "He's my dog now."

The evening turned into a fun ceremony while Babbs relayed details of staying on the vibe trail. I caught on right away it was wrong to say "we cranked the vibe." The vibe cranks itself. You have to be humble when you scout the fun vibe. Babbs put this information across in such a gentle manner everyone knew it had to be truly so.

"Hail the fun vibe," said the crew.

"I pulled a prank with the Merry Pranksters," I said to Babbs, suddenly falling on my knees. "Can I be a Merry Prankster too?"

"Sure," said Babbs. "Let's go out in the moonlight and do the induction right now!"

39

Since the Ramada was located inside a freeway cloverleaf cluster complex, the crew was relunctant to set foot off motel property, but Babbs led us through some bushes and we unexpectedly popped out on a river bank near an elaborate flower garden, with multi-colored roses in full bloom.

"Everybody take a big whiff," said Babbs, while pointing at some rose blossoms with a large, speckled hawk feather. The feather shimmered and sparkled in the moonlight. I got sleepy right away and lay down on a grassy knoll. The full moon had an orange glow around it, with psychedelic trails. There was a roar of thunder and a cloud of dust, and *Furthur*, the original magic bus, pulled up with Ken Kesey at the wheel. Babbs led the crew around the back, and up the ladder to the roof deck.

The bus blasted off towards Interstate 5, and actually left the ground and flew into a dark, angry twister that looked ready to touch ground and create all sorts of havoc. When the black fog cleared, the bus was cruising through a hundred miles of nothing but hempfields on both sides of the road. The plants were lush with birds of all colors and sizes and descriptions, who flew up to greet us in huge flocks and they were all singing happy songs about how wonderful in was to live in a hempfield with bounty free for all, and endless food in all directions.

Furthur stopped on a cliff overlooking a lake with a view of the sunrise. There was a bonfire party going on. Krassner and Gaskin were there. So was Patti Smith talking to Bob Dylan, Julian Beck, Judith Malina, Joan Baez and the Tin Man were all having a conversation with Jack Herer! But the most amazing thing was that all four Beatles were listening to Neal Cassady, who had a hammer in one hand and a gearshift knob in the other. Cassady planted the end of the gearshift into the first, and began talking about how to scout the true fun vibe.

I found myself walking between Kesey and Babbs, the Kenmasters, headed straight for the fire and Cassasdy, as if drawn like moths to a flame. "We noticed this about Cassady," whispered Kesey. "The gearshift is the chord. The crew harmonizes because everyone is on the same gearshift chord." Kesey stopped and turned to me as if to say something really important. "Strong pot without a message is just a buzz. If you take cocaine, you'll often pick up a real bad vibe because it's traveling through those hands. Real nice dope, there's nothing wrong with it…..doesn't have to be strong. You can tell how important it is by how much energy is raised to fight it."

"Is this when I get inducted?" I blurted.

"Don't you know?" laughed Cassady looking straight at me for the first time. "You're always been a Merry Prankster in your heart. You don't need no stinking induction!"

Everyone laughed and I did too because I'd had what I wanted all along and never knew it. I also felt embarrassed because I'd been so overly caught up with the money situation, just trying to break even to keep the ceremonies alive that I lost sight of the ceremonies. But now I instinctively understood if you want to hold a true counterculture ceremony, admission must always be free.

Next thing I knew, I was asleep on the riverbank underneath a rose bush, almost alone, only the dog Cassady watching over me like a guardian angel. On the way back to the Ramada, I found a large, speckled hawk feather, and it remains in my straw cowboy hat to this day.

Magic & Religion

The Secret to Enlightenment

"Harmony is the key to the universe" —Confucius

Many people make the mistake of thinking religion is something handed down from God, manifested on earth by a chosen prophet. By design, that sort of thinking turns every other religion into a false culture, making jihad not only possible, but transforming jihad into an honorable ceremony of death. In fact, spirituality can be found in all things, good and bad, and one man's noble cause is another man's holocaust. All these systems run on magic, no matter what they tell you, or what side of the fence you're on, and magic works under basic principles, most of which are obscured to keep mud in the water and keep their magic working on you without you realizing it. Magic is the original form of mind control, and if you know too much about it, you can slip off the leash. The first step to enlightenment is realizing all religious services are, in fact, magic ceremonies, and although ceremonies can have many forms, the most common form are ceremonies of harmonization, designed to create a group telepathic mind among the participants in order to focus energy into an idea, icon, symbol or concept. The tools used in these ceremonies take on telepathic power as a result of the meditations. But that power only works on those who believe in the ceremonies. If you don't believe, there is no magic. It's basically the same whether you're sitting in church or going to a live concert to hear your favorite band. Both are magical ceremonies.

One of my satori moments came while visiting my primary spiritual teacher, Stephen Gaskin, when he said: "You know, Steve, enlightenment is not like climbing a mountain or ringing a

45

bell. It comes and goes. Sometimes you're enlightened and can stone people with your presence, and sometimes not."

The idea of an individual retreating to a high mountain cave, meditating for years, finding enlightenment and returning to civilization is a false myth, although such meditation may be necessary to quiet a manic mind. One thing about spirituality, there will always be scores more fakers and frauds than real messiahs. We found that out the hard way in the 1960s, a decade that brought out the craziest of New Age cults. I ended up sticking with just a handful of elders: Stephen and Ina May Gaskin, Ken Kesey and the Pranksters, Paul Krassner, Wavy Gravy, Plunker, these titans emerged as my spiritual teachers.

When it comes to mind control, the basic sigils are father, mother, hero and devil, plus a lot more after that, but none really have the resonance and power as those top four. Devil has a lot of faces, like infidel, but you know it's the dark side, which always implies violence is an option. The messiah-hero comes to rescue you from the devil's influence, although for some he also can get violent in the process, as this encounter is often a staged dialectic designed to lead the opposing sides into conflict. Gearing people up for war has always been a huge part of mind control. When I was reading the *Rig Veda* for the first time, I couldn't help but notice how many prayers were devoted to psyching troops up for impending battle.

Mankind has been walking through the same basic scenarios for centuries, and it's safe to assume the powers behind the scenes intend to keep things this way. Some people seem to think religion was created to lead people to enlightenment? Not really. Religion was created to mind control. The minute you start believing the dogma, your subconscious sigils have been rearranged, and whoever controls your religion controls you (all religions have power centers, and all power centers either emanate from evil or

46

eventually attract evil over time). See, the devil often comes cloaked in a messiah's sigil, and it's pretty easy to set-up mind control ops around religion. It happens all the time.

Dark side, light side, no big deal, either side works equally well and you can join the insiders' club that runs the world from either direction. They don't really care about your dogmas and they certainly don't care about goodness or purity or virtue, the only rule inside this game is big dog eats first. The insider club can be entered either from darkside or lightside since both options cannot exist without each other. Both sides of this dialectic have dogmas and mind control formulas, just sign up and listen to the master while he rearranges your internal psychic center of energy. Don't matter if the master is the Pope or Albert Pike or Billy Graham or even Mark Passio.

Here's the real secret to life: anyone can manifest any energy they want if they learn how to channel psychic energy. Just build an altar and direct your mind wherever you want (instead of letting the masters direct your mind for you). When teenagers fill their rooms with posters of the heroes and goddesses they worship, they transform the room into an altar and put energy into those icons and also receive energy back, especially if that icon becomes a sigil in their subconscious.

Most people don't need my advice on how magic works because these energies move naturally through us all, whether you know it or not. But when you put up those posters (or build that altar), you're actually praying to those spirits, and that's how that energy comes into you. Pray for what you want, and learn how to build ritual and ceremony that directs your psychic energy exactly where you'd like to go, hopefully with as much emphasis as possible. I promise you will get there. And all this praying doesn't have to look anything like a church service, by the way. It can look more like a rock'n'roll party, it's still the same psychic

47

energy and energy comes in all sorts of flavors. Just know where you want to go. Figuring that out seems to be the biggest problem for many.

The recent film *The Secret* is really just a bland retread of Napoleon Hill's incredibly effective insights. Without knowing anything about him, I've been practicing some of these strategies most of my life, starting when I visualized myself into a garage rock band at age 15. Hill was a journalist sent to interview Andrew Carnegie, and that interview changed his life. Carnegie convinced Hill success in business could easily be achieved by virtually anyone, provided they followed a few simple rules involving telepathic energy. A lot of Carnegie's insights are surprisingly similar with my concepts on energy, or, as others like to call it, spirituality, although I've only recently stumbled onto these insights through Hill's book. The basic concepts include the ability to form group telepathic mega-minds capable of visualizing a path to success while banishing all thoughts of failure.

Just as Carl von Clausewitz wrote extensively about the telepathic energies of war (fog, friction and centers of gravity), Napoleon Hill outlined the telepathic energies of success in business. This only happened because Carnegie encouraged Hill to visit hundreds of successful people and document the similarities of their strategies for success. The result became one of the top ten best-selling books in history: *Think and Grow Rich*, published in 1937 after 20 years of research. It's not really a book about making money, however, but about how to architect a telepathic environment that assures the success of any endeavor. Ken Norton attributed his success against Muhammad Ali in 1973 to having recently read this book. (*Think and Grow Rich* is in the public domain and can be downloaded in pdf form from a variety of sites.)

Something Heavy Went Down in Jerusalem

Every now and then, something really heavy goes down in the telepathic energy fields we call spirituality or magic, since they're both the same thing. I noticed that in the mid-1960s. Although I'd been raised in the Lutheran faith, I rejected Christianity at the age of 14 and never looked back. In my quest to uncover the real meaning of life, I began experimenting with cannabis and LSD, after which I was never the same, as these substances helped deprogram me. Soon, I had a whole new field of sigils cooking in my psyche, one of the most important of which was the Prankster Magic Bus Furthur.

Since these sacraments had a profoundly positive effect, helping to strip away years of brainwashing, I could see why they were so prohibited. Something heavy went down in California in the 1960s, and a lot of the New Age cults (like Scientology) got their start off that energy, yet broke the cannabis connection almost immediately. I remember reading Tom Wolfe's account of the Merry Pranksters. Wolfe was a Yale grad, a real oligarchy insider who could never connect with a scene so steeped in new telepathic energies, so he just made fun of hippie spirituality because those energies never reached his soul. But there was something real and heavy going on, even if Wolfe couldn't make contact. Just like something heavy went down in old Jerusalem.

Did you ever consider cannabis was the spark of both spiritual revolutions? I remember when I first met Jack Herer. He was obsessed with decoding the Bible, a trick he'd recently learned from reading John Allegro's work. Jack would read a verse from the Old Testament, and then explain how it was really just a code for an old priest about to sodomize a young initiate. I never got into this research because I view the Bible as science fiction anyway, so why would I pay much attention to any of its possible underlying meanings?

I wonder, though, why haven't some Muslim activists taken Allegro's work and made a YouTube video about the potential spiritual corruption embedded in Judaism and Christianity? Funny thing about the spiritual revolutions of both Jesus and Johnny Griggs: one took place 2,000 years ago, and the other took place nearly 50 years ago, but they both could have easily been ignited by cannabis. And somewhere along the line, the corrupt priesthoods (because all power centers start corrupt or corrupt over time) broke this link between cannabis and this great spiritual awakening and the two sides have been at war ever since. And it wasn't until my generation that massive amounts of young people began slipping off the mind control orchestrated by that corrupt priesthood. And it all started with cannabis, Kerouac and rock'n'roll .

Music and Magic

Music is a key element in magic, or as some people like to call it: spirituality. Magic and religion are the same thing and always have been. When a tribe forms, it feeds on telepathic energy and ceremony, ritual and a sense of enchantment are used to focus and amplify the communal spirit. In the past, a tribe decided what sort of energy they were going to celebrate. Today, the state has taken over that role, and if you look around the media, you can easily see our real state religion seems to revolve around Satanism and the dark side. Which is not to say the people running this system are involved in that sort of worship necessarily, although they could be, only that their mind control program involves shifting youth over to the dark side, making it easier to pit us against Arab fundamentalists. In the sixties, we were headed in the opposite direction, so you have to wonder how the whole movement was turned 180 degrees with such apparent success?

Music has always been a huge part of ceremony and ritual…and mind control.

Hymn to Apollo

The picture above is an inscription of the famous hymn to Apollo that was sung just prior to battle in early Greece. You can actually listen to a recreation of this hymn, a Paean that sometimes decided a battle before it was even fought, so intensely did it alter the psychic field of combat after being sung by thousands of Greeks ready to lay down their lives.

In the minds of most Greeks, Apollo was connected to the Oracle at Delphi, whose magic reigned supreme at the time. For some Apollo may have represented the father sigil. He was obviously a masculine energy suitable for war, but he would soon morph into a messiah figure for future generations, and eventually even turned into Jesus Christ. Apollo was not, however, exclusively the god of war or even associated with the dark side, that would have been Ares or Hades, much harsher dudes, who probably would have inspired much different scales and melodic styles (more dissonance for sure), just as the Beatles sound a lot different from Metallica. According to Wikipedia, this first-known example of music and warfare has the following construction:

"The First Hymn is in the cretic (quintuple) meter and in the Phrygian and Hyperphrygian: an archaic pentatonic effect is produced in the lowest tetrachords by avoiding *lichanos*, while above *mese* (nominally middle C) there is modulation between a

51

conjunct chromatic tetrachord (C D♭ D F) and a disjunct diatonic one (D E♭ F G), extended by two more chromatic notes, "A♭ and A."

And if you can follow that, you know a lot more music theory than I do.

The amazing thing is that Satanist Death Metal is actually used as the soundtrack on the iPods of the soldiers at war these days. These are not prayers to Apollo, my friends, but prayers to Satan. It sort of makes me uncomfortable, but then I can't watch my kids play shooter video games without squirming and running from the room in horror, and I'm sure a lot of kids are playing Death Metal while playing shooter games these days, getting ready for the day when they can have a blast doing the real thing with real blood splatters (and if that doesn't work out, they can don their battle gear and shoot up the local movie theater with their iPod playing their favorite hymn to Satan). A lot of our media is actually designed to help people kill people. See, unless you're a psycho or longtime user of SSRI's, killing people runs against your deepest instincts. So before you go to war, it's best if you get re-programmed, otherwise the post-traumatic stress is going to wreck your life anyway. Even more disturbing, the same music is used as torture at Guantanamo Bay prison, a site that has been created to brainwash and prepare MKULTRA robots for ops for the next 30 years, no doubt. It's all part of the evolution of the science of torture and mind control. If they weren't using death metal, it could just as easily be Sesame Street or Wagner or anything else. You just have to play it loud enough so that the person being tortured can't hear themselves think, which means they can't think. After 200 or 300 days of continuous music torture, they'll introduce a messiah figure to rescue you. This figure will be used as your psychic guiding light for the rest of your life and will finally save you from the evil dude who has been physically and verbally messing with you for months. Some day that messiah may even send you on a mission where you get killed, but they won't tell you about that in advance. After you've been a useful tool in the geopolitical game of drugs, guns and manufactured conflict for profit, your mental wreckage will be easily discarded. So get ready for the names of those people tortured in Cuba to start showing up on the most-wanted lists around the world because you know that's the sort of blowback you can expect from this operation.

Introduction to Energy

All matter is made of energy, and energy systems can harmonize (tune up). When you hug or kiss someone, your two energy fields (auras) are joined into a single field. Likewise, when you sit at family dinner, the family can harmonize into a single energy field and that's one reason why family dinners are crucial in raising well-adjusted children. The earth is a self-regulating energy system. Since my definition of god is "everything" and I believe there's an energy field created by everything, I have no doubt of god's existence. In Native American terms, the Great Spirit flows through all things. It makes no difference what name you put on this energy field, the fact it's there is proof that it exists. All religions are like rivers running towards the same sea.

Energy comes in flavors. And you can channel and amplify different energies, depending on what sort of spirituality you're looking for. The hippies of the 1960s weren't called "The Love Generation" for nothing. That was the energy flavor we were seeking to amplify and share, and we learned a lot about how to manifest that energy. Mainstream culture is dominated by what I call "warrior" energy. The biggest ceremony in the United States is probably the Super Bowl. Please don't make the mistake of thinking sports isn't "spiritual." Everything in life is spiritual. If you put all the energy flavors together in one big energy stream, that's god. God is the energy that flows through all things. It's like an OM circle. When you are chanting an OM, there's no bad note. You can't sing off-key. That's because the OM embraces every note. Most ceremonies seek to harmonize energy fields. In sports, any team plays better when they are harmonized. And they all have ceremonies to help with that process. When they stand in a circle, put their hands together and chant the team slogan, they are performing a ceremonial ritual designed to harmonize. There's really little difference between those types of sports ceremonies and an OM circle. (Although I believe the OM circle is actually the fastest and easiest way to harmonize a group of people).

Energy moves through us naturally, and manifests ceremony and ritual whether you realize it or not. Science isn't really interested in telepathic energies, so little is known for sure. The real science in this area took off with the Nazi's and then was imported secretly into the CIA. The global situation is just a big game for generating profit, you see, and the players are orchestrated into position and led into conflicts that can be mined. The CIA and Foundations have spent billions studying mind control technology and mass propaganda techniques, the results of which are in constant daily use by the global corporations as they build brands while hiding secret monopolies. But most people only think of two kinds of magic: peace magic and dark magic.

Peace magic is about elevating love vibrations. Love is non-violent and never seeks control. Dark magic, on the other hand, is about bending others to your will. One is about respecting the tribe, the other about making the tribe respect you. Gandhi and his followers like Dr. Martin Luther King Jr. are peace shamans who have become so iconic they raise to messiah status, just like Jesus or Socrates. At that point, however, they have actually attained more control than any dark magician could ever hope for with his rituals of terror and violence. So the sorcerer slays the peace messiah. It's a pattern that keeps unfolding almost every generation. And it will not end until we can protect our peace messiahs while exposing the dark magicians among us.

Since WWII, using billions in resources, the Nazi art of dark magic has reached new dimensions and new heights of effectiveness, which is why when a 9/11 dark magic theory revolves around Aleister Crowley, I tend to view it about the same as those initial dark magic masonic stories around JFK. I believe we have a serious rabbit hole going on here, a blatant attempt to move the center of energy on conspiracy research away from empirical fact and into the realm where any detail can be manipulated and morphed into a sigil. It's all about connecting dots that don't really connect. These theories are a red cape being waved by a hidden bullfighter.

A big part of magic is creating and manipulating symbols. Our telepathic collective unconsciousness is a dream emanating from millions of minds, a river never stagnant but filled with evolving symbols and archetypes, or if you prefer the more magic term, sigils. This energy stream is not the same everywhere because energy consciousness is based on propinquity, intensity and the flavor of the particular energy involved. Visiting the site of a violent crime one finds a much different energy field than one finds at a Rainbow Gathering or similar peace meditation. Some of the most intense energy synergies take place during sex when two or more energy fields fuse into a single aura. But similar, though usually less intense, energy clouds form around families, congregations, communities, and even nations. The OM circle is one of the most effective devices for quickly establishing an energy field. Most ceremonies start by creating a circle so the telepathic energy flow can commence at high volume. The creation of sigils has changed dramatically since the invention of the Internet and there's a big telepathic cloud that has formed and it keeps getting bigger. It's all an important part of evolution, and the Internet is having a big impact on the evolution of our minds.

Father and mother are the biggest subconscious archetypes, and the most powerful by far, so they are the most often manipulated. In my dream world as a child, Andy Griffith, the celebrity who most resembled my own dad, was interchangeable with my own father and the two could morph into one creature at times. Long ago, the sun and moon were transformed into father and mother archetypes at the beginnings of organized religion and still retain some of that aura, but probably not much as ritual greatly evolved over the years, and the ancient pagan archetypes have likely suffered quite a beating in the process. When you spend a lot of time in church, praying to that cross or similar symbol, you're actually investing ceremonial magic into a sigil, and, at the same time, tweaking your own internal center of psychic energy.

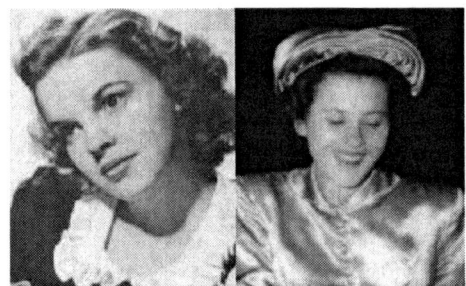

My mom, on the other hand, was often interchangeable with Judy Garland in my dreams, making the *Wizard of Oz* an extra-powerful affair.

In any supposedly democratic nation, the dark magicians in power will seek to plant the President as a father archetype, which aids domination and control by the state. But if they can't get you to buy into that game, they'll create a rebel sigil that will lead you into actions that render you powerless. The teenage delinquent meme that was manufactured in the 1950s encouraged rebellious youth to steal cars and rob gas stations for fun just when television was impacting their minds. This lifestyle was easy to contain and helped unleash random terror on the population at large. When people start organizing against war, that's when they become a real threat to these dark magicians, not when they rob gas stations and steal cars. Meanwhile, kids who don't conform continue to be programmed into violence and mindless thrill crime.

The big thing about magic: it works when people believe it, but a real serious magician, one who works on a big scale, is playing with your subconscious, so his magic is working whether you know it or not. Hypnosis and modern advertising are not that far apart.

While there are magic sigils in the mind, these sigils often also have physical representations in the real world that can become quite powerful. When an army marches into battle, they carry battle flags that must be protected at all costs, for if your pendant falls into enemy hands, or even hits the ground, your side loses psychic energy. And by the same token, the capture of a sigil during battle was probably sometimes enough to defeat the enemy's will to fight.

Think of the world as a giant go game and magicians of all stripes are constantly vying for territory. But there's a big dog in this fight, and his share of the board keeps increasing exponentially. These are the dark magicians who manufacture war for fun and profit and one of their biggest American recruitment centers is the secret Skull & Bones society at Yale University, a society steeped in black magic. But, then, so is the mafia, or any other brotherhood of death, only the Bonesmen are operating on a bigger scale. And while the Sicilians eventually broke down and top insiders eventually told all, not a single Bonesmen has ever broken his vow of omerta. Do you think one of them ever will? I mean, one of them who really has something important to say? I do know three successful low-budget movies have been made about Skull & Bones, so the mining of the media franchise, so important with sigils these days, has probably already commenced. Somehow, if a whistleblower ever does emerge from Bones, my first thought will be, is this guy a fake? That's about all you can hope for in this wilderness of mirrors we live in. But as Sam "Mooney" Giancana always used to say: "If you want to find the killer, see who survives.

The True Story of Adam and Eve

It's unfortunate the sacred texts from the world's religions become corrupted almost beyond recognition over time. For example, although the story of the burning bush made it into the Bible, the identification of the crucial plant did not. This plant, in fact, may have created the first big wave of modern spirituality (based on a perception of a single energy uniting all spirits). We do know fire temples were suddenly erected from Iran to India, and a medicinal plant was mixed with milk and served in a ceremonial manner. They called this plant "the King of the Healing Plants" in some quarters, in others it was known as "The Tree of Life" or "The Tree of Knowledge." Using instincts as my guide, I now relate the true story of Adam and Eve.

In the beginning The Great Spirit flowed through the light and through the air. That was the first day.

The Great Spirit flowed through the water. That was the second day.

The Great Spirit flowed through the vegetation, the seed bearing life, and that was the third day.

On the fourth day, The Great Spirit flowed through the living creatures, the animals, the birds, the insects and all the fish in the sea.

On the fifth day, Eve was born.

On the sixth day, Adam was born.

And on the seventh day, here's what happened:

There's no getting around the fact girls mature faster than boys, so isn't it obvious Eve was ready for the most important role in her life (motherhood) long before Adam was ready to set aside his foolish boyish games? It must have been hard on Eve trying to get Adam's attention so they could get busy starting a family. Eve was a sensible girl, so she called out to Mother Earth to help her find a way to get her family started. In a dream, Mother Earth instructed Eve to take Adam down to the river and make him partake of the Tree of Life that grows wild along the river banks.

And wouldn't you know it, after Adam got high on cannabis, he was suddenly a lot more susceptible to Eve's sexual charms and started to pick up on these cues for the first time? And of course, we all know the end of the story: Adam and Eve made spectacular love and then created all of us, their children.

And that is the real, true story of Adam and Eve, our great-great-great-grandparents.

Now, let's consider how this story was rewritten in today's Bible, where Eve is portrayed as vain, dumb, and evil, while Adam is tricked into partaking of the Tree of Knowledge, and then cast out of the Garden of Eden, presumably to live in the desert somewhere because "he has knowledge?" This story has been twisted beyond recognition in order to: subjugate women as second-class citizens, and encourage the peasant population to remain in a state of ignorance.

The True Story of Mount Sinai

Is Mount Sinai of the Old Testament a real place? All we know is that Moses got the inspiration to lead his people out of Egypt after traveling to the top of Mt. Sinai, where he was confronted by a burning bush that spoke to him with the voice of God. Later, after the Exodus began, Moses revisited the top of Mount Sinai to receive the Ten Commandments written on stone tablets. There has long been dispute over the origins of the words "Mount Sinai." Some believe it's a reference to the Sumerian Moon Goddess, others think it must be a volcano. Why volcano? Because Mount Sinai means "smoky mountains," and its peak is always clouded in smoke, where a fire burns continuously.

I've come to believe the smoky mountain of Mount Sinai is actually a reference to cannabis intoxication. It was only after becoming intoxicated with cannabis smoke that Moses received the inspiration to lead his people out of slavery. Today, many people recognize the inspirational powers of cannabis. For example, Carl Sagan attributed all his important scientific discoveries to inspiration he received after smoking a joint. Louis Armstrong and John Lennon also spoke of the inspirational powers of cannabis. And wherever you find cannabis use, you'll find spiritual cultures seeking to throw off the chains of oppression, whether it be Rastas in Jamaica or hippies in North America.

Cannabis intoxication began tens of thousands of years ago with the Saka culture, which was born in the Ukraine but eventually spread from Europe all the way to China and India. The Sakas domesticated horses, built the first covered wagons and spread cannabis seeds wherever they traveled. Their culture had an enormous influence on the development of spirituality around the world, replacing the concept of a world filled with spirits to a world dominated by a single energy field that flowed through all spirits. But because they had no written language little is known about them other than what outsiders like Herodotus observed.

Cannabis incense burners in China were often shaped to look like mountains, and the smoke emanated from holes in the top, as if coming from the top of a mountain. This is probably the Mount Sinai Moses visited. These bronze incense burners could be placed inside small tents in order to fill the tent with smoke. After a few minutes inside, one became intoxicated....or, as Moses would have referred to it...."one felt the power of the Lord..."

Chinese incense burner

61

Later, cannabis use would change from incense burners in tents to a cannabis-infused milk beverage. This was a more healthy and effective way to consume the medicine. This beverage was called Soma in India and Haoma in Iran.

In the 1950s, a banker working with J.P. Morgan, then the richest man in the United States, a man with very close ties to the Bank of England, wrote several books stating Soma and Haoma were made from a mushroom, Amanita Muscaria. This rabbit hole may have been created to lead people away from discovering the truth about the origins of cannabis use and its influence on the development of spirituality.

If you want to investigate this further, Chris Bennett has some excellent books on the subject, especially his tome on Soma (*Cannabis and the Soma Solution* published by Trine Day).

The Hippie Ten Commandments

1) Everything's connected (I'm in you and you're in me), so act accordingly.
2) The true Bible is written in the hearts of the people, so follow your heart.
3) Do unto others as you would have them do unto you.
4) Strive to be non-violent in thought, word and deed.
5) Do not lie, cheat or steal.
6) Heart energy is clean energy (as opposed to ego energy) so amplify your love vibrations and keep your ego in check.
7) Cannabis is "The Tree of Life" and has been since the dawn of civilization. Make the most of hemp.
8) Regarding cannabis, however: the less you do, the higher you get; strive to know when its appropriate to be intoxicated and when it's not (unless you have a medical need).
9) Honor your elders, your ancestors and your children.
10) Pass to the left.

On Magic and Religion

Anyone who claims special access to information from other dimensions is a guaranteed 100% fraudster. This hoodwink is nothing new, by the way. It's been going on for centuries and never seems to fail to capture true believers. In fact, this is how all religions start out. When spirituality moved from tribal shamanism to organized religions, the first thing the corrupt priesthood did was claim a special relationship with god. All religion is really magic. You can claim your messiah's miracles are really real, but there isn't any fundamental difference in the way Christianity, or Scientology, or Mormonism, or Aleister Crowley actually works—it's all magic. And magic does work—if you believe in it, so it's pretty much self-fulfilling. And most magic is based on bell, book and candle.

I don't doubt that telepathic energies exist, and some of those energies may even travel through the dimensions of time and space. Also, some people, usually known as "psychics," can occasionally tap into telepathic energies. A good example would be George Washington Carver, who had the ability to "talk to plants." But for every real psychic there's always been ten thousand fraudsters, all claiming special access to hidden knowledge they will happily share with you—for a fee. Why anyone would ever believe any of this hogwash is beyond me. One thing about real psychics like Carver: they don't use their abilities to manufacture religions or profiteer in any way from their special talents. And if they did, they'd likely lose those talents right away. So please don't make the mistake of thinking the ruling elites have any special access to other dimensions or worlds in outer space or are really lizard creatures from another dimension. This is simply a hoodwink story made-up to justify their monopoly on power and keep the populace in a state of shock and awe, and prevent them from realizing the truth—that people have the power. It's just a matter of waking up and shaking off the mind control mechanisms being manufactured to prevent that global wake-up from taking place. And claiming the Illuminati have contact with other dimensions is not part of the solution, but just another rabbit hole leading to nowhere.

The Master Mind

Congo Square, birthplace of the counterculture

The most vibrant cultural movement of our time was founded in Congo Square, New Orleans, because that was the only place in North America where anyone could mix and forge new ceremonies. On Sundays, use of the square had been set aside for the French-African slaves, who'd been transplanted from Haiti after a revolution broke out there. These slaves welcomed the Houmas natives, who probably had the best drums and undoubtedly reminded the Africans of their own tribal heritage. Congo Square was an appropriate name for this place because it was also the only place where slaves and Indians could legally play drums because they provoked fears of an impending attack throughout the original Colonies. The site had been used for years by the Houmas to hold harvest ceremonies and was considered a sacred spot. There may have been some sort of drum circle or jam session going on at Congo Square every day, but Sunday afternoon was the peak moment when the best performers went off. Congo Square created blues, jazz, rock'n'roll and reefer smoking. This culture traveled up the Mississippi, eventually infecting Memphis, Kansas City, St. Louis and Chicago. When it hit Chicago, a Jewish teen named Mezz Mezzrow jumped onboard and the rest is history.

One of the most important things I learned from cannabis: the more diverse your gene stock, the more vibrant your F1 hybrid. The Great Spirit That Runs Through Everything loves diversity and shows this affection in many ways. The reason Congo Square erupted with such creative energy is because so many diverse cultures were mixing ritual and ceremony to create a unique hybrid that respected all cultures. When you visit Mardi Gras you can clearly see the deep appreciation for Native American tradition. As blues evolved into jazz, elements of Western culture (like harmony and orchestral instruments) were incorporated. The foundation of this culture was always based in improvisation, whether it be in music, dance, slang, or gesture. The counterculture encourages freedom in every aspect, which is why every generation looks and talks different, yet all grow from the same trunk.

The most important influence in the early sixties came in the form of a Magic Bus of Merry Pranksters. Ken Kesey went from celebrated novelist to customizing his jeans and encouraging total freedom, similar in many respects to Julian Beck's cry of Paradise Now!, only the Prankster version initially involved taking LSD as often as possible, a lifestyle that quickly proved unsustainable. Acid was too powerful and potentially dangerous, although it proved to be a great medicine for those who used it sparingly. If anything was learned in the sixties, it was that reefer is the only safe daily sacrament.

Divine meets the Cockettes

The most influential group to emerge from the Haight (aside from the Grateful Dead) was a commune called The Cockettes. After the Pranksters called everyone to council, strangers began creating instant communes in the Haight that mixed people from all backgrounds. One of these communes was super eclectic and included a few gays, who were really glowing at the time because this was their coming-out party after centuries of oppression and they encouraged everyone else in the commune into dropping acid, dressing as wild as possible, and channeling whatever energy emerged. The Cockettes launched a lot of different styles, but Glitter Rock was their most important. They blazed a stylistic trail soon followed by the New York Dolls and David Bowie, among many others. They also created the cult movie scene, because their original performances evolved out of dressing up and attending a local cinema, where they used the film as a

66

sounding board. Before long, the film element was discarded as the audience was more interested in the Cockettes, so their improvisational antics became the entire show. If the Club 57 crowd had lived in the same commune 24-7 they probably would have fomented something huge, although in a way that's exactly of what happened when Keith and Kenny moved in together. Andrew Carnegie and Napoleon Hill would've called that forging the mastermind, one of their many telepathic keys to success.

The one lesson I'd take away from this is that there's probably a relationship between the diversity of a Master Mind group and the amount of creative energy that group will eventually unleash.

And isn't it interesting that our dominant religions work against these laws of nature, encouraging bigotry against other cultures and declaring jihads and crusades against the unbelievers? That's because war is a profit stream constantly being mined for revenue, so the accepted religions need to do their part to manufacture the conflicts.

Charlie Manson's OM war with Wavy Gravy

After serving 22 months in the Army, Hugh Romney attended Boston College on the GI bill and ended up studying the newly emerging improvisational theater movement (created by Viola Spolin). After college, he moved to Greenwich Village to become a comedian and was initially managed by Lenny Bruce while sharing an apartment with Tom Paxton and becoming close friends with Bob Dylan.

Before long, Romney moved to California and joined Ken Kesey and his band of Merry Pranksters. But when Kesey fled to Mexico under threat of arrest, fellow prankster Ken Babbs hijacked the magic bus Further, leaving the rest of the Pranksters stranded in Los Angeles. Romney soon discovered a nearby hog farm in the mountains was looking for a caretaker. In other words, a free place to stay. He set up a commune and called it The Hog Farm, which overnight became one of the most famous of the 1960s hippie communes.

Charles Manson drove out to the Hog Farm one day in the late 1960s. He arrived in his all-black tour bus. Manson had already made contact with one of the Hog Farmers, Shirley Lake, whose daughter Diane would eventually join the Manson family. After arriving at the commune, Manson gave Romney the title to his black bus and then tried to seduce Romney's wife Bonnie Jean (today known as Jahanara) in a nearby shed. He was undoubtedly planning on merging his family with the Hog Farm and usurping Romney as the leader of the commune. Romney managed to break up the seduction and Manson retired to his black bus with his female followers in tow. Sensing Manson was channeling the wrong vibes, Romney gathered his troops and began an OM circle next to the bus. The OM circle is an ancient ceremony from India that may have originated with the original Soma cults (See "The Soma Solution" by Chris Bennett, published by Trine Day). I believe it's the best way to harmonize a group of people and ward off negative energy. The OM circle initially became popular with the Brotherhood of Eternal Love in Laguna Beach, and was later taken up by Allen Ginsberg, who used it as a force field to protect himself and others during the riots in Lincoln Park during the Democratic convention in 1968.

Suddenly, Manson burst out of the black bus, holding his throat, choking, followed by his female followers who were quite alarmed. They tried to stop the OM circle, as they believed it was killing their leader. Manson began leading his group in an evil OM to ward off the vibes coming from the Hog Farmers. Eventually, Romney was able to persuade Manson to drive away and not return. The following year, Romney would change his name to Wavy Gravy and become famous as the emcee of the first

Woodstock festival. Manson's family would soon become the most famous serial killers in the world.

Today, Wavy remains a master of improvisational theater, which involves a deep understanding of spirituality (energy). Improvisation can unblock energy clogs and release deep inner insights. If you ever get a chance to attend a Wavy Gravy improvisational workshop, jump at it. You won't be sorry.

Manson, meanwhile, remains in a maximum-security prison and had a parole hearing in 2012. When he entered prison, Manson listed his religion as "scientologist." He kept an E-meter at his ranch. Many believe Scientology was created by military intelligence as a brainwashing and mind control operation.

The British offshoot of Scientology (The Process Church) ran an operation to capture prominent rock bands into their fold and became perhaps the scariest of all the creepy vibe masters that began to infest the counterculture immediately after it took hold of the younger generation, who'd just wiped away years of conditioning and propaganda with just one acid trip.

Ron Stark was affiliated with The Process Church and he went on to become the biggest connection for the Brotherhood of Eternal Love. Ron Stark, the Process Church, the Brotherhood of Eternal Love, these are all fascinating threads I hope to get into in the future.

Violence is black magic

When I was in high school, the thought of a teenager coming to school with an automatic weapon and opening fire on his fellow students did not seem very realistic. Even though we had students in my class with obvious mental health issues, no one exhibited the sort of out-of-control violent behavior that has almost become expected now in America.

In the 1960s, a new culture tried to emerge, one that represented a rejection of violence, but sadly that culture was so ridiculed and despised by the mainstream that it was quickly co-opted and practically erased off the earth. Ask any teenager today what he thinks of "hippies" and the answer is not likely to be very complimentary.

Meanwhile, the amount of violence pornography in our culture continues to accelerate. Just turn on any TV on any night and check out what movies are available. The overwhelming majority will be filled with gunshots, graphic beatings and senseless deaths. There's so much violence in mainstream culture that I can hardly stand to watch TV anymore since I have little interest in watching violence pornography.

Can you imagine the sort of world we'd be living in if the hippie culture (and not violence) had been celebrated and respected by mass media? Instead, the media taught our children that hippies were dumb, dirty, shiftless and lazy. Not to mention addicted to illegal drugs. Meanwhile, half the country is now addicted to pills that create mania for about 10% of users. Mania leads to psychosis. And psychosis leads to paranoia. Paranoia can lead to violence. That's why I say we have created "a perfect storm" by allowing guns for all and pills for all. Don't expect this situation to improve anytime soon.

I have some suggestions for how to deal with the situation, if anyone cares to listen. Non-violence needs to attain the same level of respect in our society that violence currently holds. To achieve this goal we need more ceremonies of peace and we need to harmonize religions in order to disarm them. My concept is not to create war on religion like Karl Marx or Bill Maher, but help religion evolve so we can ditch their dogmas without losing the ritual enchantment they provide. Almost all our major ceremonies (like the Super Bowl) are celebrations of warrior culture. I respect warrior culture, and it certainly exists for a good reason. But we have lost our balance and gone overboard with warrior worship. The peace people also need to be respected. And right now, this isn't really happening.

So bring back some of the magic of the 1960s. It's been nearly 50 years since that alternative to mainstream society's values appeared, and it's about time for that culture to make another run at transforming society. Writing this book may provide a path for some in the future to revive these vibrations.

I didn't plan to become a stoner. In fact, I was a sporadic user of recreational drugs most of my life. It wasn't until I moved to New York City in 1979 that I got tempted. But a funny thing happened on the way to that forum: After I discovered the deep connections between cannabis and spirituality, I got empowered and began manifesting ceremony like crazy.

The initial vision had been constructed around hemp being essential when this country was founded, yet the symbols (or sigils) of our founding fathers were under the control of the radical right wing, unfair and inaccurate to say the least. So I launched a campaign to create a wave of awareness that George Washington and Thomas Jefferson were actually devoted hemp farmers, and that hemp could save the world by replacing oil, a concept that had recently been introduced to me by Jack Herer. I flew out to Jack's home in the valley and laid out a plan for a national hemp legalization group called the Freedom Fighters, based around the Boston Minute Men, who would help rebuild the cannabis rallies across the country that had practically disappeared. With the hemp information, and the connections between cannabis and spirituality, I felt Jack and I might be able to rebuild that movement, with Jack as the leader, of course. "And I want you to come to the Rainbow Gathering with me," I told Jack. Both Rainbow and the Dead scene had considerable overlap, but I knew Rainbow was the real center of energy on hippie spirituality, while the Dead shakedown scene was tainted around the edges by junkies. Probably, I also wanted to pull Jack out of hard drugs and bad food, only one of which I was successful at.

Freedom Fighter parade at the 1990 Madison Harvest Festival.

The first year I hit the rally circuit I was dressed in a psychedelic shirt and tri-corner hat and carried a snare drum, but by the time the next season came around, I was wearing a brain-tanned leather outfit made by Agatha, and, on my head was a huge top hat with a pink psychedelic peace sign painted on the front. I was wearing Agatha's Native American warrior outfit and beating a round Native American drum with a peace sigil painted in psychedelic paint and chanting some Native American-type chant to Mother Earth (yes, I guess I *was* trying to move the energy from a father sigil to a mother sigil) and I was leading this immense parade down the main drag of campus-town in Madison, Wisconsin, with Chef Ra at my side, when some student jutted up and asked, "Are you a shaman?"

See, a lot of us are into magic long before we even realize what we're doing. These energies move through us naturally, so as I stood there for a few extra beats, I was thinking, am I a shaman, political activist, or guerrilla street theater performer, or what they hell am I? Pretty soon, I decided if I was a shaman it was time for something really bold, something with even more immense vibe than this 20,000-person rally. If I could just reassemble the greatest masters of the sixties revolution, you know, the Gaskins, the Pranksters, the Hog Farm, Paul Krassner, John Trudell, John Sinclair? And that, my friends, is what my magic is all about. Planting positive ceremonies in your orbit that manifest enchantment through telepathic energy.

New Children's Prayer

As an infant, I was trained to get on my knees every night by the side of my bed, clasp my palms together with fingers extended upward and say the same prayer every night. Only I always had a queasy feeling about that prayer…."if I should die before I wake." Why even bring up that concept? Something just didn't feel right. I mean, don't you get what you ask for?

Can you imagine if millions of kids went to bed every night in that same position across the world saying: "Now I lay me down for the night, I pray my friends will never fight, a day will come we'll all live in peace, and war and violence finally will cease."

How long would it take to manifest world peace if we got something like that going in a major way for a few decades I wonder? I doubt many of the religious institutions will pick up on this idea, however, much less spread it to their congregations.

Guardian Angel *by Pietro da Cortona, 1656.*

I was in the 6th or 7th grade when my older brother finally clued me into the fact our Lutheran upbringing was basically a Santa Claus story. I was absolutely furious. "Why the hell didn't you tell me sooner?" I snarled. I felt like I'd been walking around acting a fool believing some white-haired dude lived in heaven and was watching over me? It shattered not only my religious faith, but also my faith in my parents to tell me the truth, although my mom was real sheepish about the whole fiasco when I confronted her and said she'd only pretended to go along to please my dad's parents who'd grown up in south-eastern Kansas. They went to their graves believing in that white-haired dude in the clouds.

I didn't deal much with religion or spirituality for a long time after that and was basically a punk for many years with no moral foundation. It wasn't until I was sitting on the hill on Yasgur's

74

Farm that I finally got zapped. Probably Wavy Gravy helped that process since he was the main emcee and what a wonderful job he did.

But the 1970s was a terrible time for my generation, at least those of us that choose to fight against the establishment. We were herded off on a trail to nowhere, and gradually watched our entire scene diminish and fade away. But it didn't fade away. Around 1990, I went to my first National Rainbow Family Gathering, and plugged back into that spirit I'd felt at Woodstock in 1969.

I went to a lot of gatherings after that and even organized some on my own, only I called mine the World Hemp Expo Extravaganjas (Whee!). I had started the concept with the clinical "World Hemp Expo," but Ken Babbs advised it would be far better with another "e" on the end. The fun vibe was my main trail at the time and always had been as it had been implanted by my fun-loving father. Babbs and Wavy were both Pranksters on that vibe, although Wavy just dropped in for a brief time before starting his own group, the Hog Farm, and his vision was more spiritually evolved and more about service to others than having fun.

When Abby from *Daily Beast* interviewed me, I started talking about the people I've known and studied under, a list that includes John Cage, Julian Beck, Jasper Grootveld, Ken Kesey, and Wavy Gravy. This is basically the who's-who of improvisational ritual theater, the art form they pioneered and I struggle to keep alive even though most people don't know it exists and some claim I'm a fraud mouthing mumbo-jumbo and have no art at all? Abby had never heard of Wavy Gravy, but I think she did recognize John Cage. Maybe not.

Anyway, after I started going to gatherings, I'd usually be the first one up on peace meditation day, usually a Sunday, or in the case of the national gathering, always on July 4th. There'd be silence throughout the camp that morning until noon. I'd be the one who got up before dawn, however, in order to be the first at the peace pole, so I could sit there for hours, burning incense, taking a few hits of pot, but focused on one thought: praying for an end to violence and the suffering it creates. I know both John Lennon and George Harrison approached meditation the same way. When they discovered it, they'd chant for hours until both lost their vocal cords and had to stop.

Does this meditation have any positive effect? Well, it always leaves me feeling cleansed and energized. I'm always very sad to leave the natural world after living in a forest as an environmental monk for a few weeks. And I look like a road dog for a few days before I morph back into my Babylon identity.

The Real Story of 420

The 420 code for marijuana was started by students at San Rafael High School in 1971 and spread through their friends and younger siblings at the high school. They were fans of the New Riders of the Purple Sage, and often stopped by the Grateful Dead headquarters located near the school to see if any new releases were available. (Jerry Garcia was the original pedal steel player in that group, although he stepped aside to make room for the king of pedal steel, Buddy Cage.)

The annual Grateful Dead tour had captured the center of energy on the counterculture, and kept their winter home in San Rafael, after having moved out of nearby Haight-Asbury after junkies and under-covers ruined the scene. An entire gypsy caravan of merchants followed Dead tour around, many of them also living in Marin County over the winter. Sometime in the 1980s, one of these merchants made a 420 product, most likely, a 25-cent button or sticker. When this button sold out, other merchants got hip to the fact the teenagers in Marin County would buy anything with

420 on it. Meanwhile, the Waldos had long since graduated and moved on and they celebrated 420 for many years, often on April 20th, although their devotion to pot was fading somewhat as many got married and started families.

But in the mid-1980s, teenagers began spontaneously gathering on Mount Tam on April 20th at exactly 4:20 PM. This gathering only lasted three years however, because police ended the celebration as they did not want a massive display of weed smoking going on in the park.

This might have been the end of the 420 phenomenon, except that in 1990, a crude flyer designed to draw people to the Mt. Tam ritual was brought to the High Times office. This flyer had been distributed at a Dead show in Oakland over the Christmas holidays. Honestly, that flyer may have played a part in killing the annual event because the Dead scene was totally penetrated with under-covers and pretty soon, the Mt. Tam ceremony was over.

But when I saw that flyer in 1990, a light bulb went off in my head. I knew Mt. Tam was a very spiritual place, one of the most spiritual spots on the West Coast, in fact. I'd also recently been zapped by attending my first national Rainbow Gathering, which had demonstrated peace magic was alive and well, just completely ignored by the mainstream. I latched onto the idea that this Mt. Tam ritual was a spontaneous spiritual emanation of my culture and something truly meaningful that could be used as a tool to help the legalization movement. It takes a long time for a tribe to birth a religion, but eventually, over decades, rituals and ceremonies fall into place and eventually become written in stone. Its funny how a lot of the new developments in the counterculture, however, have come from kids around age 16.

So I started doing a daily 420 ceremony with my staff. We would get high and then talk about anything we wanted. These conversations ended up improving the magazine immensely as well as improving office morale. I'd started the Cannabis Cup as a low-budget event, and had not even attended the last four, instead a different High Times staffer was sent over. But issues had developed at the last one, and for the 6th Cup, I returned with some ideas about how to expand and spiritualize the event. I was bringing my concepts for 420 ceremonies as well as new trophies by Robin Ludwig.

Jack Herer was at that Cup, but when I held a circle at 4:20 PM at the venue, Jack had no idea what 420 signified. And he'd been a vendor on Shakedown Street for a decade, only he lived in LA, not Marin, so that just goes to show that 420 was not well-known inside the Dead community outside the Bay area. It was primarily a thing for teens growing up in Marin. Since my first Cannabis Cup 420 ceremony fizzled (we had a lot of tension that year at the event and little harmony), I came back the next year and my ideas were a bit more thought out.

On my way to set-up the first expo venue (Pax Party House), I ran into a guy named Eagle Bill who was carrying a wooden staff. In case you didn't know, "Pax" means "peace" and I couldn't have imagined a better venue. Arjan of the Green House had found it and it was located near his only shop naturally. That first real 420 council was a powerful event. We used Eagle Bill's staff as a council feather and passed it around to signify the speaker. Ben Dronkers, Arjan, Eagle Bill and I all spoke from the heart. Mark Emery was there and would go home and write a scathing review of the "hippie spirituality." That was the first indication I got all was not harmony inside the pot culture and some people didn't want tribal councils or the spirituality that comes with them.

The year after that, for the 8th Cup, Stephen Gaskin was brought in for the first 420 address. Stephen handed out free joints and then gave an hour-long introduction to non-violent philosophies and concepts about spirituality. Alex and Allyson Grey were also there that year. Rocker T started holding 420 AM ceremonies at the Quentin Hotel, where all the staff was located. At first, I was against this idea, as I wanted the crew well rested so they could work endless hours chopping wood and carrying water, but I did see the benefits of holding a 420 AM ceremony after the awards show. This soon became everyone's favorite ceremony at the event.

Everything seemed to be going well, but the more successful the magazine and Cup became, the more others wanted to step in and take charge. In my usual fashion, when surrounded by negativity, I opted to go home. One of John Holmstrom's columnists, a porn writer named Mike Edison, took over for a brief time. His big idea was "Potzilla" which was designed to come out in conjunction with the release of a new version of Godzilla, but the movie flopped before the magazine came out and Edison's career hit a sandbar.

For a few torturous months, I was brought back in an attempt to guide Edison and maybe even teach him something. Unfortunately, he rejected everything I brought to the table. When the Martin Luther King assassination came back in the news after a civil jury found the government complicit, I offered to have an expert in the field write an analysis of the case as it currently stood. Edison said nothing new of any importance could possibly be added at this point in history. He had no clue about deep politics or the role played by citizen researchers over the last fifty years.

I broke a major story at the time when I uncovered the creators of 420, the Waldos. But when I came back to the office with video evidence proving their case, Edison dismissed it as one of my fantasies. He'd already banned my 420 office ceremony, forcing me and my staff to leave the premises every day in order to hold our favorite ceremony. He did not like pot, preferring harder stuff and decided the Waldos were fakes and got others at the magazine to agree. Denver is the center of energy on 420 today, but that can always change. All I've done is promote non-violent spirituality as part of 420. Marijuana is the sacrament, but the culture is about living without the constant threat of violence. Marijuana, music and mathematics are the building blocks of spirituality, just as bell, book and candle are the basic tools for ceremony and ritual. I have no dogma: do want you want, as long as nobody get's hurt.

I promote peaceful, improvisational culture because I'm sickened by the level of violence being pumped out by the mainstream, and can barely watch many popular TV shows and films these days. If others like me will somehow put our energies together, perhaps we can build a less violent future for our kids. But I know this is not going to be easy.

First 420 at Rainbow

I first met Jack Herer at a NORML conference in Washington, DC. The introduction had been arranged by Doug McVay, who had given me an early manuscript by Jack that eventually turned into his groundbreaking book. There wasn't much of a chance for us to connect at the NORML conference because Jack and John Sajo were focused on their initiative in Oregon. When I tried to interview Jack, he told me to interview Sajo instead and disappeared into an elevator. But shortly after I returned to New York City, and Jack returned to LA, I booked a ticket to visit him out West. We met at a plush house with a pool in the back. This was not Jack's pad, but something more upper middle class. We sat around the pool while I ran my tape recorder and went through Jack's life story in 45 minutes or so. Then we moved back into the kitchen to smoke a joint and drink some ice tea.

The author and Jack Herer on the Hemp Trail in 1994.

While in the kitchen, I out-lined my scheme. I needed Jack to join a hemp legalization group I'd created through a cartoon character named Ed Hassle. What started as a goof, however, had suddenly morphed into a viable foundation for a national hemp movement with hundreds of ready volunteers. I'd had a vision of activists marching into rallies as a Colonial-style fife and drum corps wearing tricorn hats and flying Colonial era flags. "We need you as a member of The Freedom Fighters," I told Jack. "By dressing up in these outfits, we're more likely to get on the television news, and if we get interviewed, we talk about the history of hemp." Jack agreed to wear the outfit.

NORML didn't support rallies at the time, mostly because news photos of ragtag hippies didn't project a suitable image for forging a broad-based coalition. There was always somewhat of a divide

81

between the Grateful Dead clan, epitomized by Jack, and the more conservative factions inside NORML, most of them lawyers, and a few undoubtedly felt the hippie era was over. I was willing to work with both sides, but bringing back mass rallies was key if we were going to educate the nation about hemp saving the world.

It took Jack a year to arrive at the Hash Bash in Ann Arbor, Michigan, one of the last surviving pot rallies of any significance. But by 1986, the Hash Bash had dwindled down to a half-dozen die-hards, and they were worried the event was about to become extinct. So Ed Hassle wrote a column asking everyone to come to the event. Not only did we need to rebuild the Hash Bash, but we needed to bring back other pot rallies in neighboring states. A young activist named Debby Goldsberry emerged from the University of Illinois and created a national hemp tour in 1989 out of her vehicle. Doug McVay had begun working at NORML and provided Debby with support for this venture. In 1990 Jack joined the Hemp Tour.

Meanwhile, The Freedom Fighters rolled into the Vermont Rainbow Gathering, but tensions in the camp prevented harmony and Jack wasn't there to help harmonize. I ended up building a Hemp Education Booth and handing out Cannabis Cup matches with Alex Grey artwork. The following year, the national was in Colorado and held at a much higher elevation. There was a long, uphill march to the site, followed by a long down hill march. I got pretty tired on the way in and pitched camp midway to main circle, on a ridge overlooking the gathering. I put my tent up in a small patch of trees and started erecting signs and flags. Jack trailed in near dark with seven people in tow, none of whom carried camping gear or even a warm coat. Once it got dark, they started wondering how they were going to survive the night. I suggested they keep close to the fire. Meanwhile, Jack had a medical emergency that began with something he ate and escalated from there. He'd forgotten to bring his ulcer medication but didn't provide that essential info not to me or any of the CALM healers for two days, so no one could figure out how to heal him. I ended up taking a hit of acid to stay up all night to help take care of Jack. It was me and one other brother feeding the fire to keep Jack's entourage from freezing to death.

Since our location was on the trail, we drew big audiences to our daily 420 ceremony and took advantage of the natural amphitheater that had attracted me to the spot. One brother saw my 420 sign coming in and got really excited. I guess he was from Marin, because he wanted to name his tea kitchen 420 and encourage people to gather there to smoke pot, but was worried that might conflict with our ceremony. "That's ok," I assured him. "Just let people know Jack Herer and Steve Hager are doing a 420 ceremony here every day. The major part of our ceremony was a sermon on hemp by Jack, who was still polishing that rap. I'd already developed a rap on 420 representing our holiday, one for celebrating non-violence. I also had a theory that the counterculture began in Congo Square.

When the Freedom Fighters marched into the Diag in 1989, Jack was with us wearing a tricorn. Dozens of people had already joined our fledging organization due to full-page ads in *High Times*. I saw Steve DeAngelo standing on the steps as we paraded in, flags unfurled and drums beating. He was beaming and later told me our entrance was the best moment of political street theater he'd seen in decades. The Diag ceremony happened at high noon, so we always had to find a nearby site for our 4:20 council, where the Freedom Fighter of the Year was selected by voice vote.

Here's some little-known history of 420 ceremonies: They started with the Waldos in 1971, and passed to the next generation in Marin County, where April 20th ceremonies on Mt. Tam at 4:20 PM occurred for three years before park rangers shut down that ceremony. But from 1992 until at least 1998, I was the only person I know who was advocating and organizing 420 ceremonies. And I was promoting those ceremonies everywhere I went. If Jack Herer was alive, he'd tell the true story about the origins of the hemp movement and how the Freedom Fighters spread 420 because he's the only one with me on the mission from the start. What I find so strange is how my side of the story never seems to make it into the national media, which is constantly being filled with bogus stories about the origins of 420.

Improvisational Ritual Theater

In the 1960s, the idea of joining an experimental theater troupe was a noble concept pioneered by The Living Theater on the east coast and the San Francisco Mime Troupe out west. I studied theater as an undergraduate but was mostly initially obsessed with Anton Chekhov. I had a theory most productions were badly directed and failed to appreciate Chekhov's sense of humor, as well as his ability to poke fun at distinctly Russian personalities. Since American directors had little contact with those Russian personalities, Chevhov's plays became drawn-out with long, pregnant pauses and bombastic emotions, instead of the light comedy the author had intended.

However, I did become fascinated with the saga of The Living Theater, and would soon learn about Jasper Grootveld and the Provo Movement in Amsterdam. Julian Beck and Judith Malina had drawn the audience into the play, and loved nothing better than ending a performance with the entire audience stripping naked and then maybe going out into the street to perform an ritualistic OM circle around the local draft board. But The Living Theater was quickly hounded out of the country and forced into exile in Italy. They were considered that dangerous. Grootveld, meanwhile, had a much different fate. Today, we know him as the founder of "the happenings," and he's considered a performance artist. But his performances were intended to provoke his audience into action, which is exactly what happened. Dressed as an African shaman, Grootveld threw a flaming hoop over a statue in Spui Square during certain special evenings. Marijuana is legal for adult use in The Netherlands as a result of these ceremonies, and that, my friends, is real magic in action.

Boy, did my mind get blown when I finally met up with Andre Gregory's Manhattan Theater Project during their visit to the University of Illinois around 1972. Their version of *Alice in Wonderland* was the greatest adaptation of that novel ever achieved. The company also produced a version of Chekhov's *Seagull* unlike any other production I'd ever experienced, and one that solidified my belief Chekhov was misinterpreted. Gregory is a Harvard grad, by the way, from the Adams House, once home to head jocks, but later a center of student activism. Gregory learned a lot from Jerzy Grotowski, who re-invented experimental theater through the use of extended improvisations combined with intense yoga and mudra exercises designed to open up all seven chakras to full power. Gregory and Grotowski were really in a class by themselves at the time, both masters of what I call Improvisational Ritual Theater.

Another part of this tradition that gets frequently ignored is Ken Kesey and the Merry Pranksters, who were pursuing very similar art at the time. The Acid Tests were a deeply spiritual endeavor, as well as an artistic statement and Kesey was a pioneer in performance art as well as master shaman and magician. The Pranksters, however, were surfing the fun vibe, while Grotowski, unfortunately, seemed completely humorless, which was probably his tragic flaw. I think you can understand the similarities and differences by just realizing one was based in Poland a few miles from Auschwitz, while the other was based out of Haight-Ashbury.

It's strange how this tradition has largely disappeared from the planet. I keep the flame alive, however, when I get together with the Temple Dragon Crew. We manifest ceremony, ritual and improv energy for days, and frequently take that ball of energy to a big stage and show it off.

10 Sacred Spots

1) Congo Square, New Orleans. This is the actual birthplace of the counterculture, where Native Americans, African slaves, and a wide mixture of European whites first gathered to create an improvisational culture blending elements of all their histories to create the popular, non-violent, hybrid-vigor culture we know today as the counterculture.

2) Hippie Hill, San Francisco. Located at the base of Haight Street, just steps from the corner of Haight/Ashbury, Hippie Hill was the ceremonial gathering place for the birth of the hippie movement.

3) Laguna Beach, California. Just as important as Hippie Hill was the influence of John Griggs and the Brotherhood of Eternal Love. There is a little-known surfer-hippie connection that has not been fully explored yet. Surfers who took LSD early in the sixties were among the first people to reach true enlightenment.

4) Woodstock Festival, Bethel, New York. The first Woodstock was a true gathering of the tribe, and a place where the counterculture first realized itself in enormous numbers. It was our hippie version of the Sermon on the Mount. Also worth mentioning is Magic Meadow, Woodstock, New York. Located near the start of the trail to Overlook Mountain, Magic Meadow is the main ceremonial location selected by early beatniks and hippies who flocked to Woodstock as a haven for counterculture

spirituality. Overlook Mountain also had a long history of use by Native cultures as a primary site for vision questing.

5) Strawberry Lake, Colorado. Located on the continental divide, Strawberry Lake was the site of the original Rainbow Family Gathering. The authorities tried to close all access to the site when they learned ten thousand hippies planned on camping there over the week of July 4th, but despite the roadblocks and police presence, all the hippies managed to sneak into the site via the back trails.

6) Owl Farm, Woody Creek, CO. Home of a great shaman now departed, Dr. Hunter S. Thompson, whose widow constructed a powerful labyrinth on the site of where her husband's ashes are scattered.

7) Camp Winnarainbow, Laytonville, CA. Wavy Gravy is the foremost master of ceremonies of the counterculture and he built the second most successful counterculture community in America. Wavy is the master of improv energy and channeling the fun vibe. His camp is the perfect place to send your kids to learn about counterculture spirituality.

8) Ken Kesey's farm, outside Eugene, Oregon. The original bus, Further (or Furthur) is parked here. Kesey is our counterculture version of Odysseus, and his magic bus ride was a seminal moment in counterculture history. Wherever that bus resides will always be a most sacred spot in counterculture history.

9) Mount Tamalpias, CA. The birthplace of 420 and the site of the original April 20th ceremonies. Since cannabis is the primary sacrament of the counterculture (and has been used since its birth in Congo Square), the birthplace of 420 will always be a most sacred location for the counterculture.

10) National Rainbow Family Gathering. Every July 1-7, the gathering is held in a different National Forest so this is a mobile sacred spot that moves around every year. The Rainbow Family is the heart and soul of the counterculture. Everyone needs to make a pilgrimage to this event at least once in their life to see what a world without violence and bigotry actually feels like.

Seven Heroes of Cannabis History

Moses circa 1800 BC

According to the Torah, Mount Sinai was enveloped in a cloud of smoke and a fire burned at its peak. It was here that Moses discovered the burning bush, which was undoubtedly cannabis. After inhaling the smoke, Moses was convinced he heard the voice of God. Unfortunately, after the Roman Empire seized control of Christianity, all references to cannabis were removed from the Bible, and though the story of the burning bush remained, its true identity was completely obscured.

Zoroaster circa 600 BC

This Iranian prophet may have been among the earliest magician/astrologers. He also popularized the drinking of the sacred Haoma, a plant that grew wild along the riverbanks and was mixed with milk to achieve psychoactive results. Today, many informed scholars would admit this plant was cannabis, although traditionalists still dispute the considerable evidence.

Gautama Buddha circa 486 BC

The founder of "The Middle Way" which avoids the extremes of behavior that the east has become famous for, Buddha lived for years on cannabis leaves and seeds while meditating on the true nature of enlightenment. In the Tara Tantra, Buddha claims cannabis is "essential to ecstacy," something that is now a scientifically proven fact.

Herotodus circa 440 BC

The original Greek historian may never have imbibed cannabis in any form, but he did write the only surviving accounts of the history of the Scythians (aka Sakas), who were named after the tool they devised to help them harvest their beloved cannabis crop. The Sakas were nomadic people who roamed from Europe to the Far East, spreading cannabis seeds wherever they traveled. They began by inhaling cannabis smoke in small tipis, but eventually learned to mix the flowers with hot milk to make Soma

or Hoama. Without the efforts of Herotodus, little would be
known about this early stoner culture.

Jesus circa 1 AD

Whether he existed as a person, or just a concept, there can be
little doubt that the original Jesus movement involved a return to
the holy anointing oil that had been employed to inspire Jewish
leaders and guide them on a sacred path. Whether it was by
healing glaucoma or multiple sclerosis, the miracles of Jesus were
really the miracles of cannabis. The truth about Jesus was not
revealed until the Dead Sea Scrolls were discovered, the only
remaining texts from the period not corrupted by Roman
influence.

Jean Fumeux circa 1340

After the Roman Empire morphed into Christianity and
established a monopoly on religion throughout Europe, it took a
long time before a stoner culture would once again emerge, so
persecuted was the use of cannabis throughout the Christian
empire. But in France and Northern Italy, a creative band of
eccentrics began calling themselves "The Society of Smokers"
and they were devoted to writing songs that celebrated their love

of hashish. The poet Eustace Deschamps was a leading member of the society. These smokers were undoubtedly persecuted by the Catholic Church, which wanted a monopoly on written music. Soon all the midwives of Europe (who used cannabis as a medicine) would be killed as witches and possession of cannabis would be considered proof of witchcraft.

Francois Rabelais circa 1500

Educated as a monk, Rabelais eventually became one of the leading doctors and alchemists of his time. Aleister Crowley would take much from his work, including "Do What Thou Wilt." Because of the intense persecutions of the Catholic Church, Rabelais had to hide most of his knowledge and beliefs in allegories and fictionalized fantasies. At the time one could not even speak the word "cannabis," as it was forbidden to mention the plant, even though hemp rope and cloth were ubiquitous throughout Europe. Rabelais got around this ban by referring to the plant as "the Herb Pantagruelion." So important was this plant that Rabelais named the hero of his book, Pantagruel. At the end of his life, however, he finally revealed what must have been obvious to many: "the good Pantagruel…is hemp."

Hidden History of the Counterculture

"Things are worse than they may seem. Let's try my little scheme. Yeah! Dream! Some other dream." Father Yod, *Fire in the Sky*

Check out the official symbol of the Wandervogel (traveling bird) society born on November 4, 1901, in Berlin as a back-to-nature group that worshiped freedom and the spirit of adventure. Although later co-opted by the Boy Scouts and the Hitler Youth, this society was an influence on the hippie generation, at least in Los Angeles.

Eden Abez (George Aberle) wrote a song called "Nature Boy" about an enchanted lad who wanders far and wide spreading magic vibes. The song became a #1 hit for Nat "King" Cole in 1948. The song was really written about a group Abez hung out with in Laurel Canyon, headquartered at a pioneering raw foods restaurant run by John and Vera Richter, German immigrants trying to keep the original Wandervogel spirit alive. The group also included Gypsy Boots (Robert Bootzin) who opened his own health food store and would evolve into a major writer and prophet for the tribe.

My cousins knew two brothers from Flint Lake, Indiana, who went off to Los Angeles in the early 1960s to go surfing and came back looking like Buddhist monks. They spent the next ten years traveling around the country playing conga drums. The Nature Boy/Wandervogel spirit had obviously infected them.

But the most interesting figure to emerge from this scene is Father Yod (James Baker) a decorated Marine who served in WWII and founded his own organic vegetarian restaurant on Sunset Strip, a place made famous in Woody Allen's *Annie Hall*. Father Yod also created an important commune called The Source.

Father Yod had 13 beautiful young wives, many of whom bore his children and they all lived with their extended tribe in a mansion in the Hollywood Hills. Yod was driven around in a white Rolls Royce and treated like a king, although he left the details of running the kingdom to women.

I love this shot of Yod's Temple Dragons (his sons), all of whom were very well trained by their dad in bow-and-arrow as well as martial arts. Although the group worshiped peace and love, obviously nobody fucked with this commune when the Savage Sons were around.

Like many charismatic leaders of the hippie movement, Yod has been treated badly by the media, which usually paints him as a Manson-like cult leader. Isn't it weird how anyone who tries to wear a ceremonial hat is branded a fraud and "occult" cult-leader, but when the Pope puts on a similar hat, it's called "religion" and treated with the utmost respect? How organized religion pulls off this scam is beyond me. It's all magic, and it all runs on the same spiritual juices no matter who wears the big hat or what that hat looks like.

Music is a major part of spirituality and Yod built a recording studio in the mansion for his improvisational jam sessions. These recordings were sold for a few dollars out of his restaurant, although today the records are avidly sought by a handful of devoted collectors. Yod's lyrics can be difficult to decipher, but he comes off like an impassioned cross between Captain Beefheart and Howling Wolf .

James "Father Yod" Baker

The Occult Conspiracy

While most of the world divides spirituality into religion and something called "the occult," I know, in reality, both are the

94

same, and the division has only been manufactured to sheep-dip organized religion as something different from magic and mind control, which it really is.

In fact, the ritual and ceremony of organized religion revolves around the construction of sigils that help harmonize the natural center of telepathic energy manifested by all tribes. It's the same whether the Pope is doing high mass or a pagan society is doing a sunrise ceremony, and you can find some semblance of serenity in almost any culture. And, if it helps with your career, you can always change your spiritual orientation since it's all pretty much the same stuff.

So when people start talking about the occult as if it's some evil conspiracy that secretly runs the world, I have to laugh. Wall Street, the Bank of England and the Vatican run the world, and those institutions are crisscrossed with dozens of secret societies with a wide variety of ceremony and moral foundations (or lack of). But when you join the Freemasons, the OTO, or even Aquino's lodge, it really ain't that much different from joining the Mormons or the Moonies, which, I guess, do not fall under the label "occult" as their ceremonies are Christian based? That's really the logic people use to divide Christianity from Occult, when, in fact, it's the same magic and mind control. When you join these groups, you're not being led into enlightenment, or eternal life (as some may tell you) but are being hoodwinked into a male-dominated power formula of control. The complex dogmas are part of the hypnosis. There's a lot of sophisticated mind control video going on over the Internet these days. Most of it starts with hypnotic music. Then they start to construct the "Occult" boogieman, a psychological fear mechanism with many sigils attached.

As long as you hold the majority stock in any situation, it doesn't really matter what altar you pray at or what sigils are percolating in your subconscious. The big dog always eats first. The world situation is organized around insiders and outsiders. The insiders can easily bribe their way through any situation, and, reversely, are always available to take a bribe when asked. The insiders belong to many secret societies, the more they belong to, the more bribes they can capture. It doesn't matter to insiders what your religion or political persuasion might be, as long as the money flows and the situation remains undercover, the insiders stay happy. I can assure you that while the Sicilian mafia was taking control of the labor movement in America with the assistance of the oligarchy, the top figures, the tribal fathers, were not engaged in any baby killings or similar satanic actions. No, they were praying in Catholic temples every week and receiving absolution for their crimes from their church, while trying to raise families and pass their violent culture down to the next generation. They didn't need any inspiration from Albert Pike or Aleister Crowley, since Niccolo Machiavelli had already taught them everything they needed to know long before they hit these shores. Do you really think the gangsters inside Skull & Bones are all that different? You don't need Aleister Crowley's help to cross the line into a brotherhood of death; his philosophy works, but so do many others. Don't confuse the hypnotic mind control dogma with the actual magic.

But you know what? If you create an occult boogieman and start a search for people involved in Pike or Crowley inspired ceremonies at the top of the global food chain, that's a net with pretty big holes that an awful lot of insiders are going to easily slip through.

Candles are my new art medium. I sort of stumbled into ceremonial magic by accident when I started producing 420 ceremonies at events. At the Cannabis Cup I started with an elegant taper in cut-glass crystal until that fateful day when Alex Grey came to the Temple and had a vision of the seven lights of

96

cannabis. Later that night, I walked by a small shop and saw some colored pillar candles just the size and shape I'd been looking for. From that moment on, we did the ceremonies with seven rainbow-colored candles. At first, they were all the same size, placed on Soma's candelabra so they formed a pyramid. Later, after 622 lost Soma's candelabra, we started cutting the candles down to form the pyramid without a stand. And that's when we started carving and painting sigils on them.

Recently, however, I decided to make my own ceremonial candles rather than continuing to buy cheap candles composed of toxic petroleum wax. Without a doubt, the handmade candles I'm now crafting are the most amazing meditation tools I've ever encountered in my 40 years of counterculture ceremonies. I don't know exactly how or why they work, I just know the magic is real.

Most candles today are scented with the cheapest synthetics available but I use natural plant oils and always the best quality. The scents I favor include some of the most expensive on the market, like rose, jasmine and frankincense. I avoid commercial food scents and concentrate on smells that actually help open chakras. I frequently embed seven semi-precious stones into the candle sets because the stones can be saved and used to decorate future ceremonial candles or can be set into jewelry. That way a part of the energy from your ceremonies is kept intact forever. I think of these stones as the batteries that store the juice.

I find a lot of the candle magic being practiced today is backward and less evolved then the candle magic of the Catholic Church, which is a tremendous repository of spiritual energies, despite its scandals. Some witches tell you if you take a candle of such and such a color, and say such and such words, then so and so will fall in love with you, or give you that job, or drop dead from a heart attack so you can inherit the family fortune.

Yes, telepathic vibrations are real and spoken words can have deep psychological impact, but when you toss a vibe like that out it's like tossing a coin into the sea and expecting your dreams to come true. Not really much going on and probably doesn't have a good success rate.

One of the things about magic that really bugs me is that the serious books all storm through the shamanistic history of the world looking for that magic secret they can bring home and make a fortune off of. Problem is, magic only works when people believe, and the more people that believe, the more intense the magic. You can't take a ceremonial ritual from one culture and transplant it onto another and expect any magic at all. And yet this has largely been the history of sorcery and witchcraft.

After being exposed to the Living Theater, I fell into a little known art form I call *Improvisation Ritual Theater*. I believe that the counterculture is improvisational at heart. So I didn't need to study someone else's ideas about magic and spirituality (they are the same thing). I just let the spirit flow through me and tried different ways to amplify the energies, which, I learned, come in flavors, or if you prefer, frequencies.

At first, when I was organizing the Cannabis Cup ceremonies, I went to Stephen Gaskin and lived with him for a few weeks while ransacking his written material to assemble a guide to ceremonies that became the book *Cannabis Spirituality*. I figured as long as I needed to learn how to organize a counterculture ceremony, I might as well turn others on to the secrets. But the funny thing was, when I asked Stephen to prescribe me how the Cup ceremonies should be, he just said "I don't prescribe ceremonies. I just let them unfold naturally." And that's really the difference between "being spiritual" and just being. The more spiritually aware people are consciously building ceremony and ritual into their lives in order to enhance their lives and chart a vibratory course through the frequencies towards whatever vibration they seek: fun, peace, serenity, bliss is the counterculture recipe, but all cultures have a slightly different combination of vibratory flavors.

Compare that approach with say, "kill a frog and put it in a jar and go to the crossroads, draw a circle, put the frog in the center, and blah, blah blah." Maybe you know what I'm talking about. See the ones that want to help you open up your chakras and chart your personal vibratory trail, they are the real deal. The ones that try to tell you they have discovered the real secret to life and will sell you a personal mantra guaranteed to transform you….those are just hoodwink hucksters. And there's a lot more of them, than there are of us, the truly informed spiritual beings from the 1960s who picked up an immense amount of knowledge about real spirituality because our culture was based on improvisation.

The Alchemist's Apprentice

INT. Alchemy Lab.

A round white table with seven sets of seven candles set in a circle around a pile of precious stones. The room is completely filled with equipment, books, papers, and various tools of the trade. The Alchemist is busy making magic chakra candles when his Apprentice enters the room.

Apprentice
The top of this candle is messed up.

Alchemist
That's okay. When it gets named and first lit,
it might soon look like any other candle.

Apprentice
So why not light it now and fix it?

99

Alchemist
Oh, it shouldn't get lit the first time
until it gets named by its owner
on the other end.

Apprentice
How come you never let me
help you make the candles?

Alchemist
Because I have to do everything myself
as a ceremony in order to transmit my fre-
quency into these sacred objects.
I assemble the pieces,
but when it gets re-assembled by someone on
the other end and turned on and tuned up, that's
when it's full potential will be revealed.
You can't turn on and tune-up someone else's
set without affecting the vibrations. That
one broken top candle? That yellow candle?
I wonder if that candle is going to be more effective
and the fact that it's uniquely damaged like no other
can only make it more so.

Apprentice
Man, I'd just like to light up all the candles at once for a
change. I notice you hardly ever light more than one at a
time on your personal altar, and even then, you only leave it on
for a few minutes at most. When I get my altar, I'm going to keep
all my candles burning for hours and let the vibrations roar!

Alchemist
That could be dangerous.
And that is exactly why you are

not currently on the list to receive one.

Apprentice
Oh come on dad, cut the hippie crap.

Later that night, after the Alchemist is asleep, the Apprentice
creeps into the lab where the seven sets of MCC are arranged in a
circle on the table. He starts lighting them and turns on his boom
box.
Cut to:
Apprentice on top of table dancing in ecstasy with candles raging
all around him and the boom box blasting at maximum volume.
Apprentice starts kicking the jewels and candles off the table to
make more room for his dancing as he goes to the floor b-boy
style. Suddenly, a change has come over him, and he looks and
acts increasingly demonic. He erupts with a primal scream… and
then falls quickly asleep completely spent.

The primal scream awakens the Alchemist who gets out of bed to
investigate and discovers his lab has been completely trashed.

Birth of the Finchleys

The Importance of John Cage

Some people wonder how I turned out the way I did growing up in a middle-sized town in Central Illinois. They don't seem to realize Urbana, Illinois was a hotbed of counterculture activity during the 1960s. And I think I know a possible reason why.

After Jasper Grootveld launched the Provo movement and started creating "happenings" in Amsterdam, a handful of other artists in the world began pursuing similar concepts. There was Andy Warhol on the east coast, doing multimedia happenings with the Velvet Underground as his house band. There was Ken Kesey on the west coast doing acid-drenched multimedia happenings with his house band, the Grateful Dead. And then there was John Cage, artist in residence at the University of Illinois, who, for a few years, was organizing the biggest and best multimedia happenings in the world in my hometown of Urbana.

In order to understand the impact this undoubtedly had, consider the way energy fields work. For example, if a forest is attacked on its perimeter by a predator insect, hundreds of miles away, trees on the other side of that forest will almost instantly start producing chemicals to fight the insect invasion. Similarly, if a group experienced with meditation technique holds a meditation in a town square, violent crime can go down in that town for several days after the meditation. This has been proven by science. Similarly, the events (ceremonies) John Cage instigated in Urbana helped turn my hometown into a haven for counterculture thinking and creativity.

On March 19, 1965, "Concert for Piano and Orchestra," was performed, the first John Cage production at the U of I. It was conducted by Charles Hamm, with Ellsworth Snyder on piano. (Snyder would go on to become the first person to write a PhD thesis on Cage five years later.) At one point during the performance, Snyder crawled under the piano and began banging the bottom with a mallet. Some conservative members of the audience began screaming with rage. One even began throwing folding chairs onto the stage in an attempt to stop the performance. Suddenly, the violinist smashed her violin over her music stand, an act worthy of a Who performance. From there the concert turned into a complete melee, with the audience out of their seats and the performers improvising general chaos.

Despite intense opposition from some elements of the faculty, Cage would continue to stage performances at the University for several years, culminating in his grand finale, "HPSCHD," which was held at the Assembly Hall, the largest indoor venue in Central Illinois. It involved 208 tapes running through 52 tape-players, 59 amplifiers and loudspeakers, 6,400 slides (5,000 from NASA), 64 slide projectors, 40 films, 8 motion-picture projectors, 11 100'x40' silk screens, and a 340' circular screen made by Calvin Sumsion. The show included a lot of black light and fluorescent astrological designs. It lasted about five hours and the audience was encouraged to participate in the show in every way possible. About 8,000 attended, many of whom stayed for the entire five hours.

If you go to Urbana, you won't find much counterculture activity today. But thanks in large part to John Cage, this wasn't the case between 1965 and 1969.

The Turk's Head

Turk's Head was the center of gravity for the counterculture in central Illinois— until they demolished it around 1968. We assumed it was torn down just to destroy what had become central station for the emerging hippie culture. And the day after it was bulldozed, I went through the rubble in great sadness and found a silver ring with some Native-American-like etchings on it. That ring became my most powerful and longest-lasting magical possession. When I finally proposed at age 50, I passed it over as my engagement ring. That's how much it meant to me.

Inside the Turk's Head.

It was an old 3 or 4-story hotel, one built far from the railroad tracks and downtown areas so certain people could keep a low profile. Al Capone's gang supposedly stayed there, for example, when they came downstate. There were two major gangs in Chicago back then, and once they crossed paths in a cornfield near Urbana while bird hunting and turned the shotguns on each other. I don't remember if there were any fatalities. My family was well versed with the mob since my mom's uncle ran the numbers racket in Gary, Indiana, and even paid skim to Capone, far as I know. Uncle Freddy paid his way out of the game and went straight after the Untouchables came to town.

The Turk's Head building had a grand staircase leading to a big deck. This staircase became the hangout, and since it fronted

Green Street, the main drag through campus, just sitting on the steps was like being on display for all the passing traffic, and when you had a big group of hippies, there was a lot of rubber-necking going on. On the left side was Turk's Head, a bohemian-style, beatnik coffee-shop that served food at people's prices and often had free movies, like *The Wild Ones* with Marlon Brando, or a similar counterculture classic—with free popcorn. They also had a wide selection of exotic beers available. On the right was Mary Shirley's business venture, In Stitches, and also Bob Nutt's business venture, Blythm Ltd. (a name suggested by Jim Cole, for it's British flavor). Downstairs was The Leather Shop, created by a jazz drummer. His name was Glenn Conkright.

Front of the Turk's Head.

Bob Nutt soon took on had a young business partner named Irving Azoff. Originally from Danville, IL, Azof was a fraternity brother of Nutt, and they decided to hook their wagons to the garage-rock movement to see if it would take them to the stars. Only one would make it. Blythm had the bands completely under their thumb because they invested thousands in equipment and paid the band members nominal allowances until the cost of the equipment was paid off. In Stitches was probably the most fashionable rock'n'roll boutique in the world at the time. Mary's designs were always daring and spectacular. She was so far ahead of her time. The bands were all outfitted in her clothes (if they could afford it, that is).

108

Nutt would be yelling to someone on the phone, threatening to never let some venue book the Finchley's again unless they took all of Nutt's other bands, like the Seeds of Doubt, and they also had to promise not to book any band not affiliated with Blytham—since they had cleverly signed every competent high school and college band around. Blytham was establishing a virtual monopoly on live rock music in the area. Irv seemed like a nice guy. I bought some buttons from him and he was fun to talk to. Blytham had a huge collection of anti-establishment buttons for sale. Buttons were really big back then, as this was before t-shirts carried any messages.

Bob Nutt (in hat) and Irv Azoff

Guy Maynard of the Seeds of Doubt was blossoming into a real revolutionary and had a big confrontation with Azof at the House of Chin. The upshot was that the money from the rock entertainment business belonged to the people, not the rock stars and their managers. Irv really exploded when he heard that line. (I guess you know Azoff would soon evolve into one of the most powerful people in the music industry.

True Origins of the Finchley Boys

Paul plays cello.

I might never have met Eric Swenson if my big brother Paul hadn't decided to learn to play the cello. My mom wanted Paul to have the best teacher possible, so pretty soon he was going over to the Swenson's house for lessons, where he discovered his teacher (a member of the famous Walden Quartet) had a son his age also attending Urbana Junior High. Eric and Paul joined the Dramatics Club that year and got speaking roles in *A Midsummer Night's Dream*. The star of that production, however, was Brian Ravlin, who at age 13 was already an elfin creature from another dimension perfectly cast as Puck. But talent-wise Eric towered over everyone; he matured faster and developed his immense artistic energies in multiple directions at once. Unfortunately, Eric's mom was bipolar (long before any of us knew what that word meant—we just called 'em "crazy" back then.) She also had a serious drinking problem. She'd stay up all night several nights in a row, then go bonkers eventually and start banging pots and pans at 3 AM just to annoy Eric's dad. Eric told me he and his dad got so pissed they urinated on her while she was passed out on the couch after one of these all-night sessions. Eric laughed when he told the story. She disappeared one day, and you thought things would get better, but Eric quickly inherited the illness from his mom, going into rages, smashing everything in sight. He wasn't like this often, just an hour or two every month or so. His father padlocked his bedroom and let the rest of the house turn to total shit. The sink was filled with the same dirty dishes for months on end. Most of the other interior doors were broken off their hinges. You understood the depth of Eric's demons when you realized he could tear a door out of its frame. Eric stopped going to school and started eating all his meals at the local diner, Mel Roots, where his father covered the tab.

Eric Swenson

Eric had a life we all envied, following his every fantasy wherever it led, staying up as late as he wanted, doing whatever he pleased all the time. The nearby University of Illinois provided a lot of stimulus for him to explore. He was a rising star in the local community theater at 15, playing roles twice his age with ease. He developed a comic alter-ego named Swafford, named after a detested math teacher at Urbana Junior High. (Many years later, I'd stumble onto Ubu Roi by Alfred Jarry, the pioneering work of absurdist theater and realize Ubu Roi was an exact replica of

Swafford–right down to being based on a middle-school teacher of Jarry's). Eric invented incredibly complex Swafford routines and acted them out in Swafford's inimitable voice, elements of which were influenced by The Three Stooges. Some of these were so popular we made Eric perform them over and over, and they got more complex and more hilarious the more he worked on them. One of the grand episodes concerned a foreign-exchange student coming over to Swafford's house for Thanksgiving, but when the turkey came out of the oven, Swafford's immense greed was instantly activated and he quickly turns on the student in a rage rather than share his food. I remember snot flying out Swafford's nose after he removed the imaginary turkey from the imaginary oven, smelled the aroma, and then flipped into a paranoid frenzy. Swafford was the sort of character who'd stare you in the eye and say "the sun is shining" when it was pouring outside. You couldn't trust a word he spoke and Swafford was always hustling some con-job. When the Beatles arrived, Eric had become an instant fan. He liked Ringo the best, so he got a set of drums long before any of the rest of us had real rock instruments. One night in 1966 at the Tiger's Den, Eric was watching a local band with Mark Warwick, when they both discovered they were practicing to Beatles' records at home on their own. They decided to get together the next day at Eric's. They were both 16. It was the beginning of the Finchley Boys, who would eventually become the most famous garage band of central Illinois, although Eric's participation would end after just one gig.

Not Like Everybody Else

Jim Cole stopped by Eric Swenson's house and discovered this clean-cut kid named Mark Warwick on a red guitar playing Beatles, Stones and Animals songs with Eric accompanying on drums. Since Cole already had experience singing along to some of these records in his bedroom, using a hairbrush for a microphone, he convinced the two to start a band with him as the lead singer. Mark soon enlisted another guitar player (Steve Dyson) and a bass player (Tim Anderson) both of whom went to high school in Champaign.

According to legend as I know it, Tim was singing *Hey, Joe*, during a very early rehearsal when he started channeling some deep force inside. It's a song about a murder, and Tim lost himself completely while rampaging through the house, standing on furniture and jumping around. It may have been the first inclination that these young kids actually had the power to become a real rock'n'roll force. Once Tim stepped up to the plate, others would quickly follow. Eric was at the end of a tortured love affair, having just been dumped, and he wrote a weepy ballad begging this girl to come back. Cole played drums on that one.

Right away, people who were dropping by began to take notice. Among the first were George Faber and Larry Tabling, who offered to build speakers for a PA system. They volunteered to be roadies on the spot. George had already tried to start a band with his friend Bob Carpenter, but Eric's outfit was clearly on another level. Eventually, a student at the University named Bob Nutt came by to hear the band, and volunteered to be their manager after hearing one song. He booked their first gig in front of the Co-Ed movie theater on Green Street.

I don't know if they got paid, they were set-up on the sidewalk, and everyone was really nervous, but it was a huge success. Cole had tremendous sexual charisma, even at the age of 15 and clearly had the makings of a rock star. Eric, however, did not like the gig, and was not up for the rigors and realities of being in a band. He just didn't have the personality, and his moods could be a big stumbling block, so Nutt quickly located the best high school drummer in town to replace him, Michael Powers. Unfortunately, Tim was the next to go. I guess his grades weren't that good so his dad made him quit as soon as it became obvious the Finchley

Boys were going to take off. I'm sure that must have crushed Tim. But that opened the door for Larry Tabling to step in on bass.

The name of the band was lifted off the back of a Kinks album. (The original Finchley Boys were a street-gang in England who got into fights with the early Kinks.) That's Jim Cole (above) in 1967, at one of the early gigs. His version of the Kinks' *I'm Not Like Everybody Else* became the signature song of the group, and Cole sang it with a lot of passion. The lyrics spoke directly to all of us on the front lines of a Generation War that was already in full effect.

Stairway to Heaven

Mary Shirley

Early in the '60s, Lenny Bruce appeared on Ed Sullivan and performed a skit about some kids on the West Coast who were caught sniffing glue to get high, which Lenny found hilarious. Little did Lenny know, by broadcasting that story, he created a sudden interest in the effects of glue across America.

When the Finchley Boys decided to hold their second infamous glue party (there were really only two), they naturally selected the barn at Mary Shirley's as the appropriate location. Mary was a gorgeous rockn'n'roll blonde who designed and sewed her own outfits—hooded purple velvet cape and Carnaby Street miniskirt was a typical look. Plus Mary had two gorgeous sisters close to her in age. I never really penetrated their scene but once, for a huge ceremony and celebration in 1969, but the Shirley's undoubtedly captured the center of gravity on the Finchley's social life for a while. Mary was an accomplished musician on many instruments, violin probably being her best. She was also an asset selecting songs and helping transpose them, as well as letting them know which worked and which didn't. Mary's opinion was pretty much final.

Mary was a huge fan of the Yardbirds, who weren't really all that famous at the time, playing gigs in small clubs, and Mary would get her dad to drive her and her sisters hundreds of miles just to attend a show. The first time she saw them, the Yardbirds pulled her out of the audience and brought her backstage. They treated Mary like one of them and for the rest of their lives, they'd call Mary whenever they were in the area. It wasn't a gushy teen fan thing either. They weren't looking for sex and Mary wasn't offering. At 16, she could go toe-to-toe with the biggest rock stars and instantly command their respect. After Mary was done hanging out at these after-parties, she and her sisters would head down to where her dad was sleeping in the car, waiting to drive them hundreds of miles back home. It was at one of these occasions Jimmy Page asked Mary to transpose a sheet of classical music. He wanted to work the melody into a song he was writing. (It eventually became the opening to "Stairway to Heaven," by Led Zeppelin.)

The Shirley dairy farm was built on a hill at the south edge of town.

But in 1967, that hadn't happened yet, and everyone was going to the Shirley's to get high on sniffing glue for the first time. Glue wasn't like the ditch weed we'd been smoking, it actually got you high—way high. It was probably the first psychedelic experience for most of us. The first glue party was a relatively small affair arranged by Phil Mayall and attended by Jim Cole and a few others. It was held in a second-floor apartment on Green Street. But after that second party at the Shirley's, some of the Finchley's could already tell glue wasn't going to be their bag. Mayall was now known as Dr. Pheeoo and he already seemed to be close to a junkie on the stuff, sniffing morning, noon and night, and keeping a journal of his experiences. His dad got suspicious, found the journal and called the police.

Next thing the Finchley's know, they get a message that the cops know everything, and it'll "be a lot better for you if you turn yourself in." So the next day, George and a few others go down to the Urbana Police Station and turn themselves in for sniffing glue at the Shirley sisters' barn. George's mom was horrified. "Glue!" she said, "you won't even drink a coca-cola because you think it's bad for you!"

Phil Mayall

It would take another year or two before Phil completely gave up his obsession with glue. For a while, he even holed up at my place, the Den of Iniquity, and did his sniffing there. Here's Phil in England in 1970, living the high life.

Only Me

The first glue-sniffing party at the Shirley's barn may have inspired Phil Mayall to start a journal, but it also inspired Mark Warwick to write a song that soon replaced Jim Cole's "I'm Not Like Everybody Else" as the Finchley Boy's signature song.

You can tell from the artful pose he strikes in his publicity photo that Mark had quite a lot of style. His wide surfer-stripe t-shirt was considered super-cool at the time. He managed to grow some bangs and that was about it, as he was the only member of the band who submitted to haircut rules. Mark was exceptionally talented and his psychedelic masterpiece, "Only Me," expressed a firm belief in the intoxication of sacred substances as the true path to enlightenment.

Mark Warwick

It's hard to explain today, but the garage-rock movement was an intensely spiritual event, more powerful, in fact, than even our exploding libidos. And while the Finchley's were all about scouting the fun vibe, they also reached deep into their hearts on occasion. Cole could make the girls swoon with a Stones ballad like *Lady Jane* (a phenomenon Flick Ford would later call "the pooey meter), but when the Finchley's rocked hard, the band was more like an icebreaker or Sherman tank, leading our forces into the battles of the Generation War.

George Faber

It was at these shows that our tribe first realized itself. Lots of people make the mistake of thinking vibes are something controlled by individuals, but actually the most powerful vibes are group emanations. That's why great artists usually emerge from tribes. The really great bands are injected with energy from their scenes and the musicians become reservoirs of that psychic energy, which is why so many girls wanted to rub up against the them so badly. At their peak, their energy auras were clearly visible at times.

There were two paths at the birth of the '60s and Faber and Cole represented those paths perfectly. Warwick was on a similar path as Faber. Please don't think any of this stopped those guys from being best friends, and nobody was aware of these energy fields back then, but Mark's song was clearly suited for Faber, not Cole, and Faber would put some incredible spirituality into the song. He'd recently gotten a copy of a book on yoga, and was into health food and meditation. The song was so powerful it quickly moved to the encore slot, and Faber would start by assuming the famous "tree" yoga position. I'm sure some adults might have considered us hypnotized zombies, such was our devotion and zeal when whenever this anthem was played.

Mike Powers

I'd be amiss if I didn't also point out that the drummer, Mike Powers, was a tremendous part of the success of "Only Me." In fact, he opened the song with a drum solo on mallets, and eventually added a large gong. Mike would take a long solo with mallets at the climactic moment of the song. He was a important part of the song's spirituality.

Goddess with the Dark Hair

Chris Swing

Despite her many accomplishments, Mary Shirley did have competition for greatest garage-rock goddess of Urbana, 1967, and that competition was a dark-haired beauty named Chris Swing. I was walking down the hall one day when Chris and George Faber bumped into each other unexpectedly and began having an animated conversation with their immense sexual auras in full power. Man, everybody in that hall just stopped what they were doing so they could concentrate on what those two were saying. That was the main difference between Junior High and High School, the sexual hormones were bouncing off the walls once you got to High School. And having the Finchleys in my high school was sort of like having the Rolling Stones around all the time. Their charisma was that strong. But the charisma coming off Mary Shirley and Chris Swing was just as powerful! I didn't dare to speak to either one, they were both way out of my league, although Chris was going steady with my bass teacher at the time, Jim Brewer. I got completely plastered drinking beers in the

121

parking lot at the Tiger's Den one night. I'd just heard that Carole had driven off in some sports car with some rock'n'roll upper-class-man, and tried to drink myself into oblivion. Jim found me passed out in the alley. Chris got down on the ground and put my head in her lap to comfort me. That's how I woke up…with Chris stroking my hair, telling me how cute I looked. At first, I thought I'd died and gone to heaven. But then I woke up and got really embarrassed. Chris wanted Jim to drive me home, but I waved them off and started hoofing it back to Delaware Street. When the sun came up hours later, I woke up again, passed out in somebody's lawn halfway home.

Chris and Larry Tabling, bass player for the Finchley's, appeared next to each other in the yearbook

Funny how Chris Swing lived out in the country, just a few blocks from me and the Shirley's. Her mom Pat, remains a stunning beauty to this day, defying any effects of age whatsoever. Pat makes 80 look like the new 30. She had two daughters, but the little one wasn't on my radar in 1967, although that would eventually change.

Finchley Boys versus the Seeds of Doubt

The Tiger's Den was a one-story wood building located in downtown Urbana, Illinois, with a large, empty room that was used for a wide variety of functions, including weekly live music performances. In 1966, two local bands emerged, The Finchley

Boys and the Seeds of Doubt, and they were among the first bands in Illinois to be influenced by beat music and the British Wave, what we know today as garage bands. The picture above is a performance of the Seeds of Doubt at the Den with a psychedelic light show in full effect.

Guy Maynard

The Seeds may have come first, but the Finchley's sort of roared by when lead guitarist Mark Warwick wrote the first of many originals: *Only Me*. James Cole and Guy Maynard, the respective two lead singers, were the most charismatic teenagers in town, but they had different personalities. While Cole bedded what must have been dozens of the most nubile teenagers (who were throwing themselves at him), Maynard decided to save his virginity for a great love affair. Both were 16 at the time. *Only Me,* shifted the balance of power inside the Finchleys. Previously, the highlight of every performance had been Cole's rendition of *I'm Not Like Everybody Else*, during which he would prowl the stage and sometimes even come out into the crowd. Many of us were facing extreme battles on the home front and Cole expressed our intense commitment to preserve our hard-fought long hair and counterculture principles.

But *Only Me* raised the bar. Obviously written after the effects of the glue party the Finchley's had secretly held at the Shirley sisters' barn: *Only Me* championed our belief that the emerging psychedelic substances could open doors to true spirituality. I felt like I was in church whenever I heard the song. But it wasn't really Cole's style of song and didn't suit him. So the harmonica player, George Faber, took over singing it. Faber was already a showman, but he took *Only Me* to another level, eventually incorporating yoga positions and a live boa constrictor into the act. But when a minor dispute broke out between Cole and Faber, Cole left the band instantly, saying he wanted to play guitar. A few weeks later, he joined the Seeds as their third guitar player, and they probably became the greatest live act around for the brief few weeks they lasted. Cole would put down the guitar for one song: *I'm Not Like Everybody Else.*

Battle of the Bands

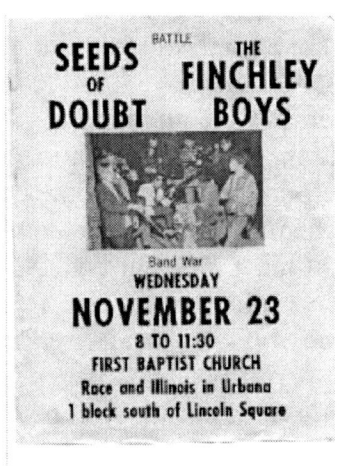

Even better than seeing a Finchley Boys' concert was seeing the Finchley's battle the other famous garage band in town, the Seeds of Doubt, fronted by Urbana High senior Guy Maynard, a very influential figure in the twin cities in the late '60s. I can tell this picture is priceless, revealing a young Jim Cole and somewhat more mature-looking Guy Maynard facing off, with their bands behind them. Within a few months Cole would have his growth spurt and morph into the local version of Bob Dylan/Mick Jagger rolled into one.

Guy was way ahead of most of us. He deplored the whole jock/longhair terminology, for example, as he knew the words contributed to the polarization taking place, a polarization that would erupt in violence in the fall of 1967, and grow worse the next semester following the Martin Luther King, Jr. assassination.

Funny, though, Guy had been a known conservative, and stanch supporter of Barry Goldwater his last year in Junior High, but when he moved to High School, he suddenly started looking and acting a lot like Brian Jones! Guy was following the first garage band in the twin cities, most, if not all of them were from Champaign Central High School. They were doing a version of *Gloria* before the Shadows of Knight, and Guy was their biggest fan. Eventually the band decided they wanted Guy to be their lead singer, and that's when they came up with the name "Seeds of Doubt."

Birth of Destructo-Mania

Bob Nutt threw a famous New Year's eve party in 1967, sort of a celebration of the fantastic success Blytham Ltd. was experiencing with their two main acts, The Finchley Boys and the Seeds of Doubt. There were cases and cases of Champagne available, a real rock'n'roll blow-out. Guy got into a discussion about "hang-ups" and decided to take off his clothes as a political statement. He walked around the party naked encouraging others to cast off their mental slavery and join his nudity. Everyone assumed he was drunk out-of-mind, but within a few months some of those same dudes would be streaking through campus while high on LSD as a political statement. Like I said, Guy was always ahead of the rest of us.

Blytham Card courtesy Guy Marnard

Meanwhile, down in the basement, Cole has discovered a hammer and spots a bunch of empty glass bottles. He turns into a robot machine and starts saying the words "destructo-mania." But every time he says the words, he robotically smashes a glass bottle with his hammer. Eventually, the host, Bob Nutt comes downstairs, sees what's going on, starts laughing and is soon joining Cole in this new game called Destructo-Mania.

It was the birth of the Destructo-Mania craze that overtook the twin cities for a few months, at least in our scene, but the apex of Destructo-Mania would not take place for over a year, and then it would be at the infamous house on Third Street where almost all the greatest parties of the decade took place.

The Monks of Mayhem

Gary Pini, photo by John McNaughton

I already told you about how Iving Azoff—the most powerful person in the music industry—got his start as Bob Nutt's associate at Blytham, Ltd., in Urbana, Illinois, in 1967. (And thanks to a Blytham business card sent me by Guy Maynard, we know Irv had a short-lived predecessor in that role.) Gary Pini is another important character in this story, and he too would eventually rise to great heights in the record industry, producing dance music singles and early rap records. Here's Gary (above) on the Quad at the University of Illinois. In the background you can see the round building we used to sneak into via the Steam Tunnels that ran underneath the entire University campus. Gary is the one who took me to see the John Cage installation at the Stock Pavilion.

Gary was going out with Caroline, who lived in a house at 1003 South Third Street with three other girls (Paula, Elke and Claudia), one of whom was an occasional lover of Jim Cole's, which is why Cole spent a lot of time at that house.

Bob Brandel,photo by John McNaughton

Cole's brother had an immaculate used Cadillac with minor issues parked in the driveway. After a few beers, Cole would go into Destructo-Mania and jump out the second floor window onto the hood or roof or trunk, inflicting as much damage as possible with his booted feet. A sledgehammer often played a role in this game and the car was soon transformed into a worthless pile of junk. Bob Brandel (above) removed the dashboard for use in an art class but flunked that project. "Why are you in school?" asked his professor. John McNaughton had a similar art class and the moldy mattress he pulled out of the Boneyard Creek so disgusted his professor that McNaughton flunked his assignment. But those two practically unknown masterpieces now constitute perhaps the finest examples of the short-lived Destructo-Mania Art Movement and would probably sells for millions at Sotheby's if anyone could find them.

John McNaughton

Destructo-Mania had to end, however, since that particular lifestyle is not really sustainable. But it sure went out in a blaze of glory. A bunch of people were tripping and drinking beer late one night when one dude sat in a chair and it broke accidentally, spilling him onto the floor. Everyone froze for a second and then broke into laughter and couldn't stop. This accident had a somewhat inspirational impact on Cole, who pretty soon smashed the nearest object with his foot. Of course, this produced gales more laughter and it sort of escalated out-of-control from there. In order to keep the laughter going, objects were ceremoniously brought into the center of the room and ritualistically sacrificed. This was Destructo-Mania of the highest and most spiritual power. No object was spared by these Destructo Monks. The girls ran around in a frenzy, moving their sacred pieces into rooms under their control, trying to save whatever they could. Small things like cups and dishes went quickly, obviously, but then even the largest pieces of furniture were eventually stomped into submission by the Monks of mayhem. And before you knew it, virtually everything in the house was turned into a broken pile of junk on the living room carpet! At this point the Grandmaster of Mayhem himself, Jim Cole stood atop this glorious pile of destruction, armed with a jack-knife and matches delivering the final *coup-de-grace*, some by sword, others by fire. By this time, however, dawn was breaking and the girls were teary-eyed, so weary were they from trying to hold back the Monks. No longer could they feed this sacred fire of destruction, as there was nothing left to destroy. So they decided to help clean up the mess they'd created and dragged the carpet with all the junk out the kitchen door and into the backyard.

Cole and his chopper, photo by John McNaughton

This house was surrounded on all sides by the most clean-cut fraternities and sororities. In fact, the backyard was really a huge

130

park used by fraternities for touch football games and frisbee throwing. The carpet was dragged to the center of this immaculate field where Cole set the mess on fire. I don't know if the Fire Department ever arrived, but I'm sure the neighbors must have wondered where that huge smoldering pile of junk came from when they woke up hours later. The next weekend, I'd kick an empty beer bottle, trying to set off another round of Destructo-Mania, but the girls threw me up against the wall, threatened to punch me out, and announced the next person who tried to break anything was getting tossed out *permanently*. It was the end of Destructo-Mania. (Another detail completely missing in all '60s films and docs: many of us were riding the new super-cheap Jap bikes. You could get a used 50cc model for $50. Here's Cole (previous page) with his chopper. Larry and I had similar bikes, as did a few others in our scene.)

The Magic Hat

Capt. Crunch Courier

The author in junior high (left).

Even though I'd been put in a special program reserved for problem kids, the best thing about going to junior high is I got to reconnect with my friends from Yankee Ridge. That's me and Steve Tyler in the front row and Andy Miller is waving his arm in the back. I joined the newspaper staff (*Tiger Tracks*) but was soon relegated to being "jokes" editor, which involved copying jokes out of paperback books and turning them in to the editor. The lamer the jokes, the more she seemed to like them.

The head alpha-male in my class was Harvey Treat, who looked like a young John Wayne. Harvey was already starting quarterback, a position he'd continue to hold all through high school. Harvey also played guitar and performed solo at one of our sock-hops. His guitar sound was similar to the Ventures, all instrumental and lots of reverb. When Harvey found out I was on the staff of *Tiger Tracks,* he asked me to slip his name into the gossip column, which I was able to do once. ("We like the way

Harvey Treat sings 'Heart and Soul' on the piano.") But when I tried a second time, the editor nixed it. She, like some of the more conservative girls in school, had already taken a dislike to Harvey I guess.

Since *Tiger Tracks* wasn't really providing much of an outlet, I soon created my own publication, *The Cap'n Crunch Courier*. (The name was taken from my favorite breakfast, which had the highest sugar content of any cereal in the supermarket at the time.) I wish I could find a copy; I thought I saved some. It was a comedy fanzine that I Xeroxed at my dad's office in the biochemistry department. My mom encouraged me to publish the paper and helped me make the copies. One of my main targets was Mr. Walljasper, the assistant principal and school disciplinarian. There were a lot of funny stories and cartoons about me and my friends. My cousins Tom and Jerry had turned me onto a new fad in California that had just emerged: skateboarding. My weekends were spent tooling around campus on my Makaha board.

Fortunately, I do have some of the original cartoons I published in the *Cap'n Crunch Courier*. I remember sitting in the lunchroom one day and I looked across and someone was showing Mr. Walljasper a cartoon making fun of him that I drew and published. I ducked down and just hoped nobody pointed me out as the culprit. Walljasper was interested in finding out who was responsible, but he never did confront me or catch me handing out copies.

When JFK was assassinated, they herded us all into the gym for a moment of silence. By the following year, the Generation Wars would commence. Some people call it the Generation Gap, but it was really a war.

Enter the Knight Riders

It sure was nice of my Yankee Ridge buddy, Stuart Tarr, to recognize my first publication, the *Cap'n Crunch Courier* (*CCC*) in his dedication to my 1965 yearbook. Things would really change quickly the next year, as the Generation War heated up and eventually boiled over. I was stuck in a program for troublemakers and had few classes with my friends and intellectual peers.

One Saturday my family went hiking at Turkey Run in Indiana, and I cracked my knee while rock climbing. I smacked it so bad that an egg-like shape swelled up and they put me on crutches for a week. Near the end of the week, however, I found myself in the second fight of my life.

137

A girl in my class was making a huge deal about what adorable teddy bear eyes I had and was debating this with the teacher and a bunch of other girls. Now, I was super shy and I thought I was going through school pretty much unnoticed by the opposite sex, so I was way too embarrassed to respond. But I saw a frown on Harvey Treat's face. And I soon heard him murmur: "He doesn't need those crutches…it's an act." Maybe Harvey had a crush on that girl; I don't even remember her name. Later in the day, in shop class, I see Harvey has his crew all ganged around and I get this paranoid feeling Harvey is talking about me. Thankfully, the bell rings and I head for my next class: band practice. I'm opening the door to the band rehearsal room, when I suddenly notice Ronald Dix standing right next to me. Ron kicks me in the shin. (Keep in mind, I'm on crutches.) Without hesitation, I kick Ron back about as hard as I could, at which point Ron lands a fist square on my choppers. I dropped my crutches, grabbed Ron by the throat, back-tripped him to the ground, and pinned on the floor. By this time, I noticed a crowd around us, some of whom were cheering me on.

"You beat his ass," said Bugsy after everything broke up. See, Ron was smaller than me, but he weighed more. He was a jock, a wrestling champ. He wore a crew cut. He was a member of the Junior Red Cross. He was as goody-two-shoes as it gets and I had no idea why he wanted to mess with me…unless it was a dare Harvey had put him on. I'd never had any dealings with Ron in my entire life.

When I got to band practice, news of the fight had already spread, plus I had a split lip and couldn't play my trumpet, so I got sent to see Mr. Walljasper, the school disciplinarian. While waiting on the couch outside his door, I started to break down. I was afraid I was going to be branded a rat and didn't know what I should say. Although it was against my instincts, I ended up telling Walljasper the truth. He called Ron into his office immediately and expressed his disappointment that a exemplary student like Ron had behaved so badly. We shook hands and Walljasper escorted us both to the gym, where a pep rally or something was already taking place. I just remember the intense shame of having to walk through there knowing the fight was being talked about everywhere. I didn't think I'd won or lost; I just felt sick at heart that I was making enemies without even trying. I was a super scrawny kid, and looked like a pushover to a lot of bullies, but the truth is, once they messed with me, they soon discovered I was a wiry son-of-bitch with a lot of heart.

The next day, the school held the final sock hop of the year, and it featured the debut of the Knight Riders, four guys from my class, one of whom was playing an organ, which was quite unusual. "Gloria" by the Shadows of Knight was my favorite song at the time, but they were playing something just as intense! I was instantly blown away and went to the very front row and bomped hysterically throughout the song. When their two-song set was over, I went backstage (the cafeteria) and let it be known I was a devoted fan on the spot and hailed them as true rock geniuses. I'd thought they wrote that song, but months later, while attending a rehearsal, I'd realize it was "Get Off My Cloud" by the Rolling Stones they were playing. I dropped the *Cap'n Crunch Courier* and began plotting how I was going to engineer myself into a rock band.

By 1967, my plan had succeeded and I was the new bass player for the Knight Riders, the junior version of The Finchleys and Seeds. We hung out with those bands when we could and were booked by the same managers (Bob Nutt & Irv Azoff). The Knight Riders introduced me to Carole, who I quickly resolved was the greatest teenage goddess in the universe.

139

Larry and the Cross

Larry Green and Doug Blair

I was sitting in the locker room putting on my street clothes when the new kid in school pointed at my Blues Magoos t-shirt and let me know how hip he thought it was. Their just-released album "Psychedelic Lollypop" included a psychedelic stencil that I'd ironed on the front of a plain white t-shirt. Psychedelic t-shirts didn't exist at this time, at least not in central Illinois, and buying that album was the only way to get one. (I still have that t-shirt today, believe it or not, as well as the leather jacket I wore through most of the '60s, although the stencil has all but disappeared and the shirt is now yellow.) I noticed something significant right away. Around his neck hung the secret sign from my Leal School gang days.

We got to talking, and I discovered his name was Larry Green and he'd just arrived from Baltimore, which I could relate to having come a few years earlier from Boston, via England and Germany. Very few kids in the school were hip to psychedelic garage rock. In fact, I thought I was the only one. Larry introduced me to Doug Blair, who soon became famous for having the longest hair in high school. Much more important, Doug had started his own legal radio station from his bedroom and was broadcasting garage rock to a significant portion of the town of Urbana. The signal was easily reached from my house as well as Larry's. That's them in the above photo, Larry on the left and Doug on the right. At the time, both Larry and I wanted long hair, but long bangs was as far as we'd gotten. It would take a huge confrontation for me to get control over my hair (see my eBook "The Steam Tunnels"). Larry soon became the first hang-out-everyday sidekick I'd had since first grade, when Bobby Davidson and I became best friends in Arlington, Massachusetts. He was a devout Catholic, which I understood, since I was still going to Lutheran Sunday school and Saturday school. One day, however, I got to talking to my older brother and discovered he and his friends at Uni High (the smartest kids in town) had all come to the conclusion religion was a fairy tale. I remember I got so mad at my brother because he hadn't told me immediately, and allowed me to continue wallowing in the darkness. Pretty soon, I told my parents I wasn't interested in going to church anymore, something that was greatly reinforced when the Pastor showed up at our house one night after dinner, attempting to arm-twist my Dad into making bigger contributions to the church. He wanted 10% of my Dad's salary, and I remember how proud I was when Dad laughed that suggestion off saying, "No, I'm not giving you that much." I made a deal with my parents. Since my confirmation was only a month or two away, once I got confirmed, I'd never have to go to church again. And I didn't. I didn't know it at the time, but the Urbana High football coach, Smitty, was a member of that Lutheran congregation, and his only son was in my confirmation class, although we seldom spoke. Much, much later in life, Larry came to visit me and handed over the cross he'd worn in the '60s, an icon both of us had invested magical powers into at one time. Larry felt it belonged with me for some reason.

*Strangely, Larry's cross was virtually identical to the sigil
I'd created for my first secret society, The Roaring 21 Club.*

The Smartest Kids in Town

There were four high schools in my hometown but only one was
really hard to get into. You had to be somewhere around 90% in
math and reading to even get considered. I couldn't get past the
math, although I did take the test. My brother got in on his second
try and soon found himself in a very special tribe.

Two of his classmates, David Goldwasser and Sam Levine, were
my age; David and I had been in the fifth grade together at Leal.
Those two were probably considered the brightest in the class, but
those dudes weren't just about brains. University High had long
been the local punching-bag in sports—it's players known
derisively as the "Uni Punys." But when my brother and his
friends started winning track meets, those words rang hollow.

Uni High was really an Ivy League prep school. They staged
elaborate Gilbert and Sullivan operettas, which provided an
opportunity to showcase their voices. Tim Peltason was one of the
ringleaders of this tribe, for sure. He'd grease back his hair and do
great Elvis impersonations. He rounded everybody up one
summer night for a long car-trip to see Johnny Cash perform live
in some fairground.

Everybody knew these guys were the smartest kids to come down the pike in a long time, and many of them were expected to go on to great things. They really dug soul music and would venture into the North End to buy blazing hot barbecue sandwiches, the only white guys in the joint. On New Year's Eve 1967, they wanted to throw a grand party. Sam was transferring to Harvard in the spring. (Sam still holds the record for youngest person ever admitted to that school.) Of course, they wanted alcohol at the party, so, in his wisdom, Paul negotiated a deal with my parents. It ended up, Paul was given a gallon or so of lab-grade alcohol to make punch with on the condition nobody drove a car that night.

Today, my Dad would go to jail, but it just shows the immense confidence and respect this tribe had generated with the older generation. They had located a huge six-bedroom, completely private house for this party, so everyone could crash there, which turned out good because there was a huge snowstorm that night. When I found out about the alcohol, I convinced my brother to let Larry and me dress-up as high-class servants to serve the punch. Paul thought that was a great idea, especially after we showed him the marching-band outfits we'd just stolen out of a closet of a church on Green Street. Larry and I got quite tipsy and had a wonderful time that night; it was probably our introduction to the positive side of alcohol. (The first time I'd been aware of people getting drunk I was in fourth grade and it scared the shit out of me. I fled that party and hid in my bed and started crying. I just wanted my 16-year-old cousin to stop drinking because I didn't like the changes I was seeing.) The climax came when one of the hotter girls in the class began weeping hysterically. I guess news had gotten out that young Sam Levine was upstairs losing his virginity.

"They are forsaking all human dignity up there," sobbed the girl.

I was thinking, "She's upset because it's not her up there, right? Otherwise this makes no sense." I drunkenly bolted upstairs and peeked into the room but couldn't see anything as they were buried under covers. "Shut the door!" yelled Sam.

Larry was way ahead of the rest of us in this regard, having lost his virginity in Baltimore at 14 or 15. He had a remarkable rapport with the opposite sex and wasn't very choosey. He liked girls of all sorts and flirted continuously. I could see how having him as a sidekick might be an asset. One last note about Sam Levine. Not only were we the same age, we had similar backgrounds. And when he left town, he gave me his cushy weekend job at the *News-Gazette*. I didn't know it at the time, but the publisher was a lover of Johnny Roselli, an enforcer for the Chicago mob who managed the Hollywood-mob connections. At the time I was a junior copy boy filing the AP wire tapes, and I had no idea Roselli was coming into town for liaisons with my ultimate boss at the paper, Marajen Chinigo. Today Sam is a world-class sax player in Nashville, Tim a leading Shakespearean scholar, Paul a biochemist, and Dave is famous because his son co-founded the band MGMT.

Paul Hager and Tim Peltason in 1968.

Reflections on Older Brothers

Since I've already outlined my teenage iconography involving the goddess side of life, it might be useful to chart some major influences on the Yang side. My two best friends, Larry and Bugsy, both had influential older brothers, both one-year older than us. While my brother was attending an Ivy League prep school, Larry's and Bugsy's brothers were living in San Francisco, the coolest place in the universe in 1967. Having a super-cool older brother gave them both a leg up on me. But those two dudes, they were as different as night and day and represented the twin paths that confronted me. And I couldn't decide which path I wanted to take and kept swerving from one to another.

Larry Green

Larry's brother, Richard, had gone South during the Civil Right's Movement and put his life on the line to help those less fortunate than himself. Richard became a full-fledged Bodhisattva, devoting himself to helping people and spreading positive vibrations. Richard came through town periodically, and instead of Champaign County ditch weed, he carried real marijuana that actually got you high. Richard turned Larry on for the first time that summer and then started driving back to Frisco. He broke down around Carbondale, and a stranger helped him fix his flat. Richard gave that stranger a joint as a present for helping him and the stranger called the cops. Richard spent a few months in jail.

But then there was Bugsy's brother, Don, who'd broken all the rules and walked the wild side since he was 14. His parents had shipped him off to Florida for a special program (probably a CIA mind control experiment—at least that's what Don and I believe today). At the very beginnings of the '60s there was already this dichotomy between the peace-love hippies, and the punks who were living in the real world of pimps, prostitutes, pawn shops and pool halls. Don was a master of that world.

Don Henderson draw by Brian Ravlin.

Here's a drawing of Don by Brian Ravlin, who soon followed Don to San Francisco. Both these brothers, Richard and Don, would soon return to Urbana, however, and I would finally meet both legends in the flesh.

Smitty and the Blaster

Warren Smith was the most famous high school football coach in central Illinois by 1958, an innovator of the Single Wing Offense originally created by Pittsburg's Pop Warner. (Single Wing was the precursor of today's shot-gun formation.)

In the early '60s, Smith invented an ingenious training device known as 'The Blaster," used to teach running backs to slip-off tackles. John Cage incorporated a Blaster into a "Happening" at the Stock Pavilion in 1968 (See "The Importance of John Cage"). Unfortunately, Smitty became obsessed with running his entire team through the Blaster, with springs cranked to near maximum. And if you got stuck in the device, you had to wait forl the next guy running full speed right behind you, to punch you on through to the other side. As a reader of this blog pointed out: "people were not designed to get slammed in the back."

Everyone called him "Smitty," except his players who just called him "coach."

Roger Ebert was a sports reporter for the *News-Gazette* in 1958, (which was then-owned by Johnny Roselli's lover—see "Smartest Kids in Town"), when Ebert wrote: "...the royal coach turned into a pumpkin, and the Cinderella Urbana Tigers stumbled and fell...": as the opening line for a story covering the annual show-down between Urbana and Champaign Central, one of the most vicious rivalries in Illinois.

Smitty blew his top and immediately confronted Ebert: "From this day forward, you are banned from all Urbana sports under my jurisdiction. You can't buy a ticket to the games." The ban didn't stick forever, but it gave Ebert a schooling on Smitty's explosive temper and somewhat fragile ego.

When I entered Urbana High after winter break in January, 1967, I was on top-of the-world. I had a bass guitar and amplifier and was taking lessons with Jim Brewer. On our annual shopping trip to Chicago, I'd been allowed to select my own wardrobe for the first time. I was wearing blue stovepipe corduroys, only the welts ran horizontal to the ground. (I've never seen another pair of pants like 'em since.) They were severely tapered to the knee, which was great, 'cause I had super skinny rock'n'roll chicken legs. The stovepipe from the knee down made them look like bell-bottoms, which had not yet become popular. Of course, once the Beatles were seen in bell-bottoms, they took over the jean market for a few years, but I had these pants years before that fad hit. I was wearing blue-suede zip-up boots with Cuban heels, similar to Beatles boots but flashier. My shirt was long-sleeved white and navy stripes with a half turtleneck. Most important, however, was the black leather jacket, double-breasted but cut shorter than a sport coat. Bugsy had found this jacket first, at Kuhn's in downtown Champaign, and it cost around $100. Very soft lamb's leather. (I wore it to the first Woodstock, then to Sweden, San Francisco and beyond; it's in my closet and fits 46 years later!)

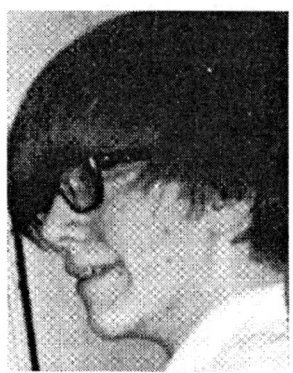

Doug Blair

But when I stepped into school on the first day in this outfit (expecting oohs and aahs from the multitudes), some chucklehead pointed at me and yelled, "He's wearing girlie pants!" This did not faze me, as I knew I was a lot cooler than that nerd.

One day, however, I was walking past the library when I heard a loud voice and some commotion and saw Doug Blair backing up fast, running into the library and being chased by some huge jock from the upper classes. Nobody was helping Doug as he danced around the stacks and ran underneath tables, trying to stay out-of-reach. Finally Doug bolted out the door and out of school. What was that about? Well, I soon learned Doug had written a paper for English class called "Smitty," and made hilarious fun of our school icon, who was already a commander in the Generation War—on the opposing side. For example: when Faber had showed up with long hair that year, Smitty had thrown him against the lockers and said, "What happened to you, boy?!"

"Maybe I found out there's more too life than running around a track," replied Faber calmly. But most people didn't dare talk to Smitty like that, and George was probably written-off as a lost-cause from that day forth, even though he was one of the stars on the cross-country team. But Doug had really crossed the line with his English paper. And it was just a matter of time before one of Smitty's devoted players would take revenge.

King of the Greasers

Across the street from Urbana Junior High was the perfectly-named Hood's Pharmacy, a one-story mini-mall with picture windows fronting an old-time soda fountain. Swivel stools, lots of chrome details, cherry cokes, and a rock'n'roll jukebox. It was your basic greaser heaven. I went in one afternoon after school, probably to pick up a candy bar, when I saw a greaser dude throw a dart right into another kid's back, causing a greaser girl to scream, "what's wrong with you?!" By the way, I don't mean "greaser" as negative in any way. In England, that style is called "rockers," and it's your basic '50s rock vibe and still exists today all around the world, centered on Elvis as the true Messiah. I stayed away from Hood's after that. It was a hangout for real hoods.

Frank Sowers

I was in the special class for troublemakers and the most dangerous characters were in there with me, so I knew who not to fuck around with, starting with King of the Greasers, Frank Sowers. I had one encounter with Frank when Stuart Vyse and I were in Lincoln Square shopping center (which had destroyed the entire downtown vibe, replacing it with the first indoor mall in central Illinois). We went to the men's room at the hotel, and while we were washing our hands Frank and another shorter kid came into the room and wanted to know if either of us would fight the short kid, who was smaller than either of us—and we were shrimps. Stuart and I both said "no, thanks," and eventually, Frank and his friend turned and left. Under his breath, Stuart stupidly says: "Son of a bitch!" and Frank immediately says "I heard that!" and re-enters the room. Stuart runs into a stall, takes his pants down and puts new meaning to the word, "stall." We looked for an alternative route out of the building, and swiftly left the area.

Speaking of tough dudes, I was having fun blowing spit-wads with Kenny Shackleford the day I met him. Eventually, I turned my aim on him and got him right on the nose. I was laughing so hard, I had to bury my head in my arms on my desk and try to compose myself. Suddenly, I feel this searing pain, and my chest collapses and I can't breath. Kenny had punched me in the back, and he had one hard-ass punch! Finally, after I could breath again, I look back at Kenny, my eyes teared up, and I see him staring me down with this incredibly angry, hostile face. Then I knew Kenny was one of those guys….the guys you just didn't fuck around with. Kenny went out for the basketball team, and Frank choose football. Kenny got killed in a North End shoot-out while still a teenager, and Frank became fixture at Rose Bowl bar and all-around local legend.

But it was Frank who decided to defend Smitty's honor. He followed Doug Blair home from school and cracked him over the head with a baseball bat. And so went the opening shots of the Generation War now being waged in public. Up until now, this war had been fought inside our homes, not in the streets and schools. But the peace in the streets was lost. Doug had the longest hair in Urbana High, and all the longhairs were plenty pissed Doug had a concussion and had to go to the emergency room. And there was really only one guy amongst us that you just didn't fuck around with, and his name was Bob Carpenter (although we just called him Carp). And as soon as Carp heard what happened to Doug, he started looking for Frank, and when word got out Carp was looking for Frank, a bunch of us started following Carp around on his mission to see what was going to happen when these two titans actually collided.

Carp Joins the Knight Riders

John Hayes before long hair

John Hayes was one of the tallest kids in my class. In fact, I think he and Harvey Treat *were* the tallest dudes their age, although Harvey was built like a rock and John had chicken legs like me. It was debatable who was more handsome, Harvey's young John Wayne or Haye's young Kirk Douglas. Hayes was blonde and had this amazing chin dimple. Hayes lived on Delaware Street, right down the block from me, so I guess it was inevitable we'd hang out at some point. But after he formed the Knight Riders and I saw their debut at the Urbana Junior High sock hop, I made it a point to start dropping by. Hayes was highly entertaining and always had great new records to listen to. One day Hayes played "Talk, Talk" by the Music Machine. We both loved the song and the black leather look of the band. Almost from day one, Hayes was encouraging me to get a bass guitar and amp, indicating I might be able to slide into the Knight Riders, as he liked my style better than his founding bass player, Donnie Perrino. I was so eager to get into a band I did exactly that, thanks to mom, who attended the auction where we purchased a brand-new 1966 Gibson SG bass and amplifier for the staggering sum of $500.

Now why John had it in for Donnie Perrino, I had no idea, as Donnie was clearly the best musician in the Knight Riders and could probably play any of the instruments better than anyone else in the band. But John had some deep insecurities because, while he was fun, he could also be cruel and vicious, and he often made fun of Donnie behind his back, which is a big no-no if you want to have any decent chemistry in your band. At the time, the Knight Riders were even rehearsing at Donnie's house and Donnie's dad was a super-cool dude and a big force in Summer Youth Music, a highly-respected program a lot of us attended. In fact, Donnie's dad Dan eventually created a hot jazz band called the Medicare 7, 8 or 9, and they became a local legend.

Donnie Perrino

But one day, Carp was on his way to give Frank Sowers a beating, and a bunch of us were following right behind. Carp knocked on the Sower's front door and Frank's dad answered. "Can Frank come out and play?" asked Carp. A minute later, Frank appeared behind the screen door. Carp asked him to come out on the sidewalk as they had something to discuss, but Frank said "no," and made it clear he wasn't coming out. This went back-and-forth for a short time, and then Carp and his entourage departed. So there was no big show-down. But we longhairs felt like we won, because Carp sent a message to every jock in school, if they were going to pick on longhairs, like Smitty was obviously encouraging them to, they'd they'd have to deal with him. And not even Frank

153

wanted to deal with Carp. Carp wasn't like a normal person. When Carp got into a fight, it was like a click went off in his head, and he transformed into a creature from another dimension capable of monstrous violence. Once you saw that side of Carp in action, nobody, but nobody wanted to fuck with Carp.

Here's another of the original Knight Riders, John Wilson in 1967, after he grew his Beatle bangs. To give you an idea of what "long hair" looked like in the fall of 1967, when we got back from summer vacation, (because that's when all the longhairs really sprouted), Wilson's blonde locks were like really long at that time. Anything that went over the top of your ears was considered radical.

John Wilson

Hayes had a real strict father, a lawyer, and devoted member of the John Birch Society (a real power in town since their leading propagandist was a professor at the University of Illinois), and Hayes had to grease his hair every morning and comb it straight back for breakfast with his dad. After he arrived at school, however, he'd wash the grease out in the boy's room and put on his regular hair-do. Since three of the Knight Riders were named "John," we usually addressed them by their last names. At some point, Hayes decided to get a lead singer, and he offered that position to Carp, and Carp gratefully accepted. But it wouldn't take long for Hayes to realize he'd just lost control over his own band.

The Magic Hat

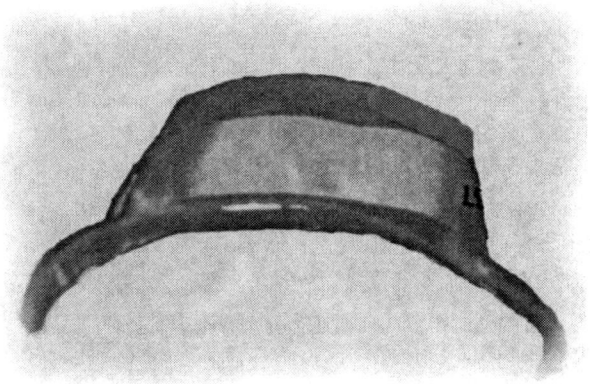

I guess you call this a porkpie, but it wasn't like any other porkpies I'm familiar with. For one thing, it had a very wide ribbon. It was blue and matched my stovepipe cords and suede boots. Lots of people said I looked like a Native American in it, which was really cool by me since I considered Natives a lot more enlightened than Christians. It had been my grandfather's Sunday go-to-church hat in Hepler, Kansas, until he'd bought a new one. I had access to one of those early letter-laminating toys, and put the letters "LSD" on the front in black. The first time I showed up for PE wearing it, Smitty called me into his office. I tossed the hat into my gym locker before going to see him. I'd never been in his office, before or since. "Don't bring the hat in here," he said.

"I put in it my locker," I explained, not quite understanding his meaning. "Keep the hat in your hall locker," explained Smitty. "Don't bring it into my locker room again or I'll confiscate and destroy it. This is your only warning." That hat *was* magic. It got a rise out of Smitty and right after I started wearing it, I found myself a member of the Knight Riders, one of the best garage bands in town.

Hayes brought me to officially meet Carp, the new lead singer. We were all going to get high for the first time. Carp had wild marijuana plants he'd recently harvested and dried and was ready to test. (Ditch weed was all over the county because a major hemp processing plant had been located near the railroad tracks in the North End. The plant later turned into a cap-and-gown factory. The reason we had blacks in our North End is because work in the hemp factory was so hard, they had to import their labor from Southern states). We smoked several joints with Carp and his then-fiance, a gorgeous goddess. (Carp would eventually go through many more, but they were both madly in love at this time and just got engaged after only a few dates).

After every joint Carp would look at us and say, "Feel anything?" I was pretty foggy just from being amongst these dudes. I can't say for sure the weed had any effect though. At one point Carp leaves the room with Hayes, and then Hayes comes back and immediately starts hitting on the goddess. Wow, was she surprised, since Hayes and I were both well-known virgins at the time. Plus, Carp had a mean temper and she knew it, and even though Hayes was trying to get her to give him a "hello kiss," she wasn't biting. On the way home, Hayes told me Carp put him up to the whole thing just to see if she'd kiss him. I guess it was Carp's way of testing if she really loved him or not. Most girls couldn't resist Hayes' movie-star looks, and Carp knew it. Hayes was laughing really hard at the idea he would do anything like that behind Carp's back. Nobody fucked with Carp.

The next day, the Knight Riders (minus Carp) introduced me to Carole, and we smoked one of those joints in Haye's car at a Uni High welcome-to-school picnic. I remember how surprised my brother and his friends were to see me show up with my new rock band! We all had fun hanging that day. I had a new mission now. Which was to make Carole my girlfriend, which might be a problem with Hayes and Knight, since I clearly detected they

156

were both head-over-heels in love with her as well, and completely under her control. I'd never been in love before and would spend hours staring at the telephone. After two hours, I might pick it up, lift the receiver, then put it back down. This could go on for a long time, but eventually I knew I would get up the nerve to call her.

One Saturday afternoon, I was pretty bored and all alone at home, when I put on my magic hat and walked out the door, vowing to do the first thing that stimulated me. A bus stopped in front of me. I had never ridden a bus in my home town before, but they had just created this new set of lines, all color-coded, that were crisscrossing the twin-cities and campus, so I hopped right on board just to see where it would take me. It took me to downtown Champaign, where I got off right in front of the big department store, where the Finchley Boys were having a show, right at that very second! I learned a big lesson about not sitting around doing nothing, but always projecting into the universe that day because, low and behold, Carole and two girl friends were attending the show and I quickly hooked up with Stuart Tarr and another dude and before I know it, a three-couple energy cloud is forming around us.

I'd already learned Carole was sort of seeing Larry Tabling, the Finchley's bass player. That news just meant I'd spend the rest of my teenage existence avoiding any contact with Tabe, even though he'd be close to a lot of my close friends. But after the show, the Finchley's disappeared, and one of the girls suggested we all go to Carole's house and make-out in the basement. Holy cow! This was it! I was in hot band, I was with the greatest teen goddess in the universe! I was about to make out for the first time in my life! I was in love with Carole! Unfortunately, I was about to blow it all, big time.....

Watch That Hand!

The Hager home on Delaware Street.

Here's the Tudor house on Delaware where I grew up. I didn't realize it at the time, but we'd been desperately poor all our lives until my Dad was made head of the biochemistry department at the University of Illinois. Suddenly our lives got a lot more plush. Unfortunately, I got into huge confrontations with my Dad while growing up. I was headed down a counterculture path by the time I turned 15, and my Dad was really opposed to that direction. I had to run away several times before I could even grow long hair. Eventually, we worked out a truce of sorts, and I moved down into the basement and began transforming it into a psychedelic playground.

Right before I moved down there, however, I'd put an Eldridge Cleaver for President poster in the second floor window of the room my brother and I shared (left corner). When my Dad saw that poster from the sidewalk, he flipped out and ran upstairs and destroyed it. I was wearing this blue hat that said "LSD" at the time, long before I actually took any LSD. I'd just gotten a bass guitar and met the most beautiful girl in town, a blonde named Carole, who lived with her mother and grandfather in Champaign. She was my age, a year behind my brother at Uni High (see "Smartest Kids in Town"). One week-end I found myself walking to her house after a Finchley Boy's concert, with two or three other couples who wanted to make out. I'd never made out in my life, and neither had Carole, far as I know. It was her girl friend's idea. When we got to the basement, we kept the lights off and everybody just sort of settled into a comfortable position in the dark. Carole said we could snuggle, but no making out. That was cool with me. I put my arm around her waist at some point and she said, "Watch that hand, don't move it any higher." I was a real stupid chucklehead at the time, and when she said that, I immediately started inching my hand up toward her breasts. I wasn't even trying to cop a feel to be honest, I was just trying to be funny. But it wasn't funny. Carole erupted immediately, and threw us all out of her basement. She was steaming mad. I walked home knowing I had just squandered the best opportunity of my life. I learned an important lesson that night. See, you have to be super respectful of girls, otherwise they won't trust you. Carole was shy and sensitive, just like me, and instead of building a foundation for a possible relationship, I'd broken all sense of trust. I hoped I could repair the damage, if I just kept working on her, which I would of course.

Photos of Carole back in the '60s are hard to come by, but I did locate this one, so you get an idea of just how gorgeous she was. Is this not the face of the Alice in Wonderland archetype that inhabits our collective unconscious?

Carole

Carole had the most incredible blonde hair. Her father's side of
the family was from the South, and she had a real Southern Belle
quality and could really talk up a storm, and had a way of
touching you while she talked that seemed like a come-on, but it
wasn't, she was just sharing her magic touch. She also made her
own clothes and was almost as good at rock'n'roll fashion as Mary
Shirley. Carole was a scholar as well; her specialty was Russian
literature and she was one of the top Russian scholars in the
country at the time, which was great, because I loved Tolstoy,
Chekhov, Nabokov and a bunch of other Russian novelists, only I
was reading translations and she was reading them in Russian.
Carole was always helping people out when she could. She spent
an hour every week reading books to blind people. Her mom was
super cool and loved me from the start, although her grandfather
was suspicious and highly protective. Unfortunately, he passed
away soon after I met Carole and that was another trauma she had
to go through after shortly after her parent's divorce. The day after
the funeral Carole had a vision her grandfather came to visit her to
tell her he was all right in the spirit world. Unfortunately, very
soon, an unexpected development would put an end to my
constant fantasies of going steady with Carole.

My First Trip on LSD

It wasn't long after Hayes brought Carp into the Knight Riders that the band began plotting how to get rid of him. Meanwhile, Tim Anderson, the original bass player for the Finchley's, convinced his dad to let him re-join a band. Tim was the first member of the Finchleys to unleash real rock energy at a rehearsal and help guide the band into the realms of real rock'n'roll—what Dave Aguilar of the Chocolate Watchband describes as: "An overloaded lumber truck coming down the mountain," to which I would add only: Riding two wheels on all the curves. Hayes held a secret tryout with Tim and we were all very impressed with his passion. "We finally got a real showman in the band," said Hayes happily. Tim left that rehearsal thinking he'd just joined a band.

"What about Carp?" I wondered. There's an age-old technique for getting rid of band members without any uncomfortable confrontations, and Hayes was naturally going to employ this technique by disbanding the Knight Riders and then re-forming a new band a few days later with Tim as the new lead singer. Of course, this new band would require a new name and Hayes asked me to start thinking up possible new names. I decided to split rather than stick around to see what was going to happen when Carp showed up for a band meeting and heard the bad news about the Knight Riders disbanding.

I hitchhiked over to the Union Tavern, in the basement of the Illini Union, one of my three favorite hangouts at the time, the other two being Turk's Head and House of Chin. (This was before the Red Herring Coffeeshop opened in the basement of the Unitarian Church.) Bugsy was sitting at a table wearing a huge Cheshire grin. An older beatnik dude was with him. I started talking to Bugsy, but the older dude interrupted right away.

"Bugsy's tripping right now," he said.

161

Holy Cow! This was the first I'd heard of any LSD in my hometown! That's when I noticed Bugsy's eyes were big as saucers. A buddy of Bugsy's had just flown to San Francisco for the weekend (the round-trip ticket was under $300), purchased several hundred blue capsules of LSD (still legal at the time—150 mics each we were told). The caps cost $1 on the street in the Haight, but could be sold for almost anything in Urbana, so desperate were people for a taste of this new substance. On an initial investment of less than $1,000 my friend was planning to make at least $10,000 in profit. I could see calculators going off in everyone's head. Bugsy fronted me four capsules for the special price of $10 each and told me I could pay him after I found a buyer. And it was all perfectly legal.

I headed over to Doug Blair's new crib. After the baseball-bat beating by Frank Sowers, Doug had left high school forever and been accepted straight into the University of Illinois. He was a straight-A student running his own radio station at the time, so it hadn't been too difficult. But instead of moving into a dorm like most incoming freshmen, Doug had located approved-student-housing on Third Street. It was a giant old house and had two or three beds in most of the rooms, but somehow Doug had scored a small private room on the very top floor all by himself.

The first time I visited, Doug had been getting high by sniffing lab-grade toluene. I tried it and almost instantly had a frightening panic attack and couldn't remember my name for about 30 seconds. It freaked me so bad, I never wanted to sniff glue again. The only earlier experience I'd had with glue was when a bunch of us decided to hold our own version of the Finchley Boy's famous glue party. We were at Jim K's house and after we got high, I ran out to his backyard, which fronted the Urbana Golf Course, took off all my clothes and started running around naked. Of course, this greatly concerned my friends, who desperately tried the herd me back inside while trying get me re-dressed. They

162

finally got me back into the house with my underwear on, when Jim K started chasing me around the house brandishing a huge kitchen knife. He wanted to stab me because he'd only hosted this party on condition that everyone behaved, and obviously I hadn't.

Fresh Cream by Cream had just been released and Doug was listening to the song "I Feel Free" when I arrived. I showed him the blue capsules and we decided to split one right away. Twenty minutes later, feeling nothing, we split another. Twenty minutes after that we decided to go to the Union Tavern and check with Bugsy.

But Bugsy was nowhere in sight. We started coming on just as we sat down at a booth. When a waiter came, we realized we had to split because he could no longer function as normal people. In a daze, we walked out on the terrace on the Union's south side, where Doug bumped into a girl he knew named Spacey. She started flirting with Doug. I couldn't communicate, so I pulled Doug aside and said I needed to return to his crib where I felt safer. I just wanted to curl up in a blanket and listen to records.

Doug guided me back to his place but he wanted to go back outside. "Don't leave me!" I pleaded. Doug came up with the idea of me calling someone to babysit me via the telephone. I thought that was a great idea, and, of course, I called Carole.

"Well, you can't have kids now," she said when I told her I was tripping. They were spreading a lie at this time that LSD caused birth defects. Funny how it took so long to reveal this connection with alcohol, but they prematurely jumped all over it when it came to LSD.

Carole secretly tape-recorded my rantings while I described all my hallucinations and sudden revelations. (She'd discover the tape many years later and tell me it all sounded so innocent.)

163

Eventually, Doug returned, by which time we both had huge psychedelic auras around our heads. We stayed up all night listening to music. Doug had the best record collection and stereo equipment of anyone I knew.

Around 8 am, I left for school and arrived at the pavilion at Carle Park across from Urbana High. The pavilion is where all the longhairs smoked cigarettes before going to class and I unexpectedly bumped into the Knight Riders. Carp had thrown them down the basement stairs and threatened to beat the shit out of them if they tried to disband so the band was still intact with Carp as lead singer. I wasn't surprised. Then I pulled a piece of tin foil out of my pocket, opened it and revealed the two capsules of LSD. The Knight Riders got very dismayed and started acting like I was a heroin junkie or something. No way were they interested in anything as powerful as LSD! A few hours later, Hayes informed me I'd been kicked out of the band for being a drug addict.

First Trip to the Haight

One night I was sitting in my psychedelic playground otherwise known as the Den of Iniquity, when my Dad unexpectedly showed up with another biochemistry professor from Berkeley, California. I guess he'd come to Urbana to give a seminar. My Dad had told him about me, and this dude wanted to meet me because he was a peace activist. He loved my paintings all over the walls, and pointed out that a peace symbol I'd painted over my desk was missing one of the spokes. That made me feel a little dumb. The amazing thing was, this professor invited me to come spend a week with him in the Berkeley Hills!

I was soon on a flight to San Francisco and I was reading all the Hobbit books at the time and was deep into Hobbit-land, which today just seems like a boring remake of WWII done with magic and elves, basically war propaganda. The first book had been great, but the trilogy seemed bloated to me. One thing you have to give the Brits credit for, however, when it comes to magic, they rule. That goes for dark magic and white magic.

I spent the first few days hanging out on Telegraph Avenue when I got recruited to help out at a people's church that a hippie pastor was setting up. There were two guys working on this project and I became the office assistant for a few days. My host seemed a bit dubious of the Christian-connection. He was an atheist and distrusted organized religions. He'd drop me off on his way to his lab every morning, and pick me up at 5:30 every night to go home, where we had dinner prepared by his beautiful Swedish wife, and then played a game of chess or two.

Watercolor by Flick Ford

One day while walking down Telegraph, this hippie started talking to me like he'd known me his whole life. His name was Jinglebells and he was originally from New York City. Jinglebells had really long hair and was wearing high-top suede moccasins with bells around his ankles. He wanted to know if I wanted to hitchhike with him to the Haight. He knew a place we could crash. This was too good an offer to turn up, so I soon found myself wandering around the Haight. After it got dark we went to the all-night church where all the runaways congregated who didn't have a place to sleep. It was really crowded. Then Jinglebells took me to Page Street to visit a commune. There was a beautiful girl who seemed to be at the center of this scene. She said Country Joe had come over the night before and sung songs with his guitar all night while everybody tripped. Country Joe had led the Hari Krishna chant for hours, apparently. There was a guy in a Navy uniform and he was hitting on a plump hippie girl. Everyone fell asleep while this couple eventually had sex on the living room rug. In the morning though, the whole vibe changed and the beautiful hippie girl was mad at us. "This is not a crash pad!" she said. I also heard her say she didn't know Jinglebells well enough to trust him. Pretty soon, I figured out she was surviving by buying bricks of Mexican weed and selling lids on the street.

Jinglebells decided to hitchhike on down to Big Sur. "It's a beautiful scene down there," he said. "You should come with me." I was sorely tempted, but decided to hitchhike back to Berkeley and walked miles uphill before I found the house I was staying at. The Swedish lady was really pissed at me and made me call her husband immediately. I made up some story about how a friend had been arrested and I'd gone to the police station and spent the night trying to get him out of jail. "Why didn't you at least call us?" they wondered. The visit was over in another day or two anyway. Things were pretty somber at his house after that incident and I guess now he understood why my Dad was so frustrated with me. But I couldn't get that close to the Haight and not at least spend one night soaking up the vibes there.

Birth of the Tin Whistle

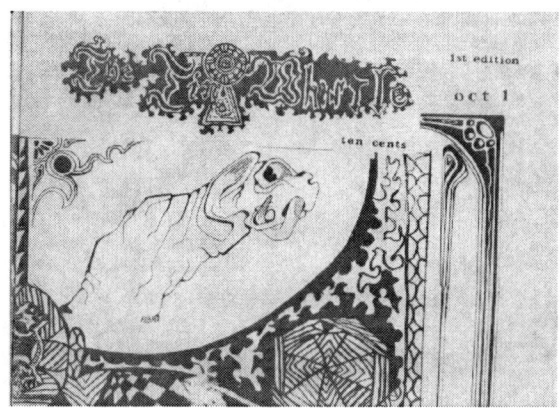

Debut issue of the Tin Whistle.

Remember I said I was reading the Hobbit series? Well the first issue of *The Tin Whistle* had a picture of Gandalf I drew (see below). I also made the first logo (above), which I think shows evidence of Hobbit influence in the weird font I devised. The strange creature in the picture above, however, was draw by Larry Flom.

Meet the first issue of *The Tin Whistle*, my second start-up operation after the short-lived *Cap'n Crunch Courier*.

It all started when I got invited to this meeting to discuss a media project, I wasn't sure exactly what. I think the meeting was held at St. Pat's Church in Urbana, but I could be wrong. There were about eight or nine people present, including, maybe Stuart Tarr and Albie Fisher. If so, they would have been the ones to suggest I attend. There was a dark-skinned dude, maybe his ancestors were from India or Iran? He spoke perfect American and was obviously raised here, and was running this meeting. I believe he was a freshman at the University of Illinois. For some strange reason, he had an interest in helping an underground newspaper get started in

167

the twin cities, and was looking for some people to take on this project if he provided the initial seed money.

Since I was the only one with any experience publishing anything, the dude eventually asked me if I was interested in running this new publication. I said sure, and he said, what name would you give it? I was holding a long, tin whistle in my hand, really just a prop for my hippie-hobbit persona, when I looked up and said, "How about The Tin Whistle?" Everybody loved that name.

I think the dude asked me how much money I needed to get started, and I said, "One hundred dollars." He wrote me a check on the spot. I never really had any contact with this dude ever again. I can't remember if I even paid him back the hundred dollars. I did have his telephone number because I called him for help one time, and he actually came running and saved me from a beating, a story I will get to shortly. However, he never expressed any interest in the content of my newspaper and just seemed delighted that he'd helped get it started. I'd like to find that dude today, just to see if any hidden agendas were in play. He looked like a total straight arrow and it was hard to fathom his interest in counterculture journalism.

I heard the underground paper at the U of I, the seldom-published *Walrus*, had an office on the North End of campus, so I went looking for it. They welcomed me instantly, gave me keys to the building and access to all the art supplies. They also hooked me up with a cheap offset printer. I had the first issue out in a matter of weeks. The *Walrus* staff was astounded. I made them look bad in a way because I'd almost single-handedly published an 8-page underground paper, while all they'd done is sit around and talk strategies for weeks on end. Eventually they would start getting issues out as well.

Before I published the first issue, however, this big black dude named Charlie Geron came by my new office. He'd heard I was going to publish an underground paper and wanted to know if he could write for it. I said "sure," not knowing Charlie would soon become my star columnist.

The Outcasts

Larry Green attacks Urbana High.

169

The first issue of *The Tin Whistle* included my endorsement for Larry Green for Senior Class president, our counterculture attempt to take over the political structure of a school that had always been dominated by the winners of the annual Daughters of the American Revolution awards. You'll notice Larry wears the magic cross that was also the secret symbol of my elementary school streetgang (see "From Violent Streetgangs to Merry Pranksters"). I took both photos the same day, cut them up and glued them together to create the effect of Larry as teenage monster towering over Urbana High. The story "Tales from the House on High Street" is an obvious reference to Eric Swenson's pad, our favorite hangout. After the Knight Riders kicked me out of the band for being an LSD addict (or so they thought), I toyed around with the idea of starting a band with Eric and we held a bunch of rehearsals at his house, but I soon came to the conclusion being in a band with Eric wasn't really going to amount to anything real, as Eric was more than content to just jam in his living room and nothing more. He always had a cigarette in his mouth when he drummed, and used an overturned cymbal on the floor as his ashtray.

Meanwhile, The Finchley Boys were going through their own changes. Somewhere along the line, they started doing an Animals' cover, "Outcast." Actually, "Outcast" was originally an R&B love song Eddie Campbell and Ernie Johnson recorded in Phoenix, Arizona, in 1964. The Animals version was faster and they dropped the horn riff and replaced it with a guitar. The song rocked hard, had a powerful hook, and it instantly became a major highlight of the Finchley's set, eventually becoming their new signature song. It was no longer a silly love song, either. Now "Outcast" stood for the position we longhairs found ourselves in, as we were not being accepted by the establishment. Faber was the lead singer on "Outcast." Although Faber had started as the roadie, then played harmonica on one song, he was now singing the two biggest hits the band had. One day when the band was arriving in a car together at Urbana High, Faber and Cole got into a little dispute over some minor matter and Cole announced he was leaving the band so he could concentrate of becoming a guitar player. Cole soon left high school and moved into a room on the second floor of Eric's house, right across the hall from the padlocked room Daddy Swenson slept in.

One day I brought Larry with me on one of my visits to Carole's house. We were sitting on the floor of her porch talking, when Larry went into his imitation of Timothy Leary. Carole started cracking up. It was the first time she noticed how smart and funny Larry was. I had this idea we should cover ourselves with a blanket and pretend we were all in a womb together, about to be born as a set of triplets. I don't know where I came up with this shit, maybe I was already aware of the Living Theater, because this was essentially an improve exercise right out of a Viola Spolin handbook. We went to the back yard, threw a blanket over us, and curled into a ball, all spooning each other. I was on the outside, and, of course, Carole was in the middle. It was all very innocent, really. But I could tell right away from the way Carole was petting Larry's hair, that she'd taken a sudden interest in him. When she went back inside, her mom was super pissed. "What are the neighbors going to think!" Carole stood her ground, however, saying we were just playing a game and nothing sexual had been going on at all, which was true.

I could see there were speed bumps ahead with my grand scheme to make Carole my girl friend, as she seemed to be easily distracted by other dudes.

Jock is Beautiful

Racism and discontent essay that helped sparked riots in school.

The first issue of *The Tin Whistle* could not have been more explosive and the first two articles in that first issue actually set the stage for a lot of what would happen for the rest of the year. "Jock is Beautiful," was written by Charlie Geron, and made reference to a beating inflicted on a prominent member of the U-Club. The blacks, it seems, had finally taken sides in the jock-longhair conflict Smitty had been fomenting, and decided to side against Smitty and with the longhairs. Charlie also took a swipe at the U-Club Parent's association, run by Smitty and the fathers of his white stars. The other (unsigned) article was titled "Racism and Discontent." "An impending crisis hangs over Urbana High School and no one really realizes the seriousness of the matter....the White racism and Black discontent that are so prevalent in our nation and community is manifested in the actions and attitudes which make Urbana High a potential area for racial disturbances." These words would soon prove very prophetic.

I didn't realize it at the time, but those two articles were extremely offensive to Smitty and he immediately called a meeting of the entire U-Club. After they were all assembled, he entered the room and exploded: "I put more niggers through college than any coach in this state!!" was just one of many comments made during this tirade.

During most of the speech, Smitty was staring straight at Jim Wilson, who was the starting end at the time, and Harvey Treat's favorite receiver. In fact, Harvey's favorite play was a bomb he threw to Jim. So far they'd run the play three times and it had scored a touchdown on all three tries. "If you see some kid with his shirt hanging out, smoking a cigarette, you have my permission to punch them out," concluded Smitty.

Although Smitty didn't actually say "longhair," I think those final comments were aimed at me and my crew. Smitty had watched me grow up because we went to the same Lutheran Church for many years, until I defected, something that would have certainly not gone unnoticed by him. The U-Club meeting was Smitty's way of declaring war on the counterculture and especially *The Tin Whistle*; and the first casualty in this war was Jim Wilson, who'd continue suiting up for games for the rest of the year, but would never play football again in his life. Such was the punishment for writing a letter to *The Tin Whistle* that Jim actually didn't write! Many years later, John Reinhardt confessed to Jim that the unsigned letter was actually his.

The tragedy was that Jim was talented enough to get a football scholarship. He placed third in the State in the high-jump that year and could basically out-jump just about anybody, a great asset for an end. He was around 6' 4" and had blazing speed. His dad, a track coach at the University, had been grooming Jim for a possible professional career, but then Jim's dad died unexpectedly, and then Smitty silently blacklisted Jim off the football team for a crime he didn't commit. Jim could have folded his cards and given up on life. Instead, he decided to run for senior class president. And you know what? Not a single member of the U-Club ran against him. I think it was an amazing display of their respect and affection for Jim. As well as their realization that maybe Smitty was wrong. But Smitty had been right about one thing: Jim was the alpha male on the civil rights movement in our class. And if he could get a chance, he intended to confront the racism so prevalent in our school at the time.

Paranoid Delusional Breakdown

Doug was a university student for about one semester before he decided to drop out of the U of I. He applied for a job as a disk jockey at one of the local radio stations and got it. Doug soon moved to an apartment near Uni High. He put an extra mattress on the floor in his two-room apartment and I was always welcome to crash there. He was still sniffing toluene at the time, although Doug had his sights set for bigger and better highs. After extensive research, he and a friend from Uni High decided the easiest psychedelic to self-manufacture was DMT and they set about collecting all the ingredients, supplies and equipment necessary, all of which was being stashed in secret panels above his kitchen cabinets. They were stealing this stuff by going into the steam tunnels and entering labs late at night (see my eBook, "The Steam Tunnels"). They would always dress up in lab coats and act like graduate students while breaking into these labs. Sometimes they would just brazenly load up carts of supplies and wheel them around in full view of anybody. The secret was that white lab coat, which gave them an aura of respectability despite their long hair.

Doug was at work during the afternoon, and I had a set of keys, so first chance I got, I invited Carole and her friend Alice over to check out my new hangout. Larry was also with us on this particular day. Doug had completely covered one wall with record album covers and he always had the best records, including lots of really obscure stuff you couldn't find anywhere else. Around this time, Doug turned me onto the little-known West Coast Pop Art Experimental Band and H.P. Lovecraft, a split-off band from the Shadows of Knight. I played my favorite cuts from both albums. The girls, however, seemed more interested in a campy "Hobbit" record that had been churned out to cash-in on that craze. It was really silly and they laughed while playing one particularly silly song over and over. It was about Daffodils.

Carole and Alice were also interested in the toluene, never having tried glue, so I showed them how that worked. Before I knew it, Larry and Alice were deep into their bags and had crawled under the covers in Doug's bed. Suddenly, Carole put down her bag and french kissed me with great passion. It was the first time I'd ever kissed a girl and my mind sort of exploded. I was super aware of the mistake I'd made the first time around, so I pretty much kept my hands to myself, while Larry started balling Alice right away. I just kept making out with Carole. She probably was wondering why I didn't make any serious moves, and she actually ordered me to get high at one point and handed me her bag. I pretended to take a few whiffs, but I really had no interest in the glue high. I was a lot more high from that French kiss. I was extremely conscious of the fact Carole was in a compromised state and was determined not to take advantage of the situation. Mostly, though, I was just a typical virgin, I guess, too shy to make a serious move. Eventually, Carole and Alice had to go somewhere and they both split rather suddenly. A few minutes later, I noticed the bottle of toluene was missing.

That's when I had the first major paranoid breakdown of my teenage existence. Before long, I'd convinced myself that the whole make-out session had been a ploy to steal drugs. I was a very sad chucklehead back then because I'd soon sabotage any potential relationship with Carole by concocting the most evil scheme imaginable. When Doug came home I told him about the missing bottle. Doug just opened his secret cabinet and pulled out a giant gallon container of toluene he had stashed there. But after I explained my plan to Doug, he readily agreed to play his role. So I called Carole and said Doug had gotten back, the bottle of toluene was missing, and Doug was going into withdrawal. I acted really crazed while Doug painfully moaned in the background. Before long, I had Carole in tears. She called Alice and Alice's story was the bottle had been tossed in the bushes or something. We never got it back. But my torturing of Carole over this stupid bottle was really over-the-top, although in my paranoid delusion, I couldn't stop myself.

Undercover informant Don Clark.

After the phone calls were over, and Doug and I were laughing about what great actors we were, Doug mentioned that the news director at his new job was a really cool guy who wanted to meet me. His name was Don Clark and unfortunately, he would soon radically change all our lives.

Race Riot at Urbana High

I was seated in the auditorium at Urbana High, waiting for the senior class speeches to begin, when Larry Green suddenly appeared out-of-nowhere wearing an elegant double-breasted pinstriped suit. "Can I borrow your hat?" he asked. "Sure, I said," tossing him my blue hat, famous around school for having "LSD" embossed on it.

I was the publisher/editor of *The Tin Whistle* at the time, and Larry was our official candidate, and I'd run a campaign promoting Larry's election. Our school was in great emotional turmoil at the time, starting when the football coach, Smitty, encouraged members of the U-Club to beat-up longhairs and Frank Sowers hit the kid with the longest hair in school, Doug Blair, over the head with a baseball bat. Then blacks sided against the U-Club and jumped on one of the head jocks in the halls. At first, that seemed like maybe a good thing. Unfortunately, it was not.

Larry wears the magic hat.

I remember standing on the second floor of Urbana High about a day later when I saw a typical violent altercation about to go down. There were around six sophomore blacks ganged-up against one prominent senior starter on the football team. But before anything could go down, a half-dozen white members of the football team appeared out of nowhere, running to the rescue from all directions. Obviously some sort of alarm system was now in place amongst the team to thwart these random beat-downs that were taking place. At that moment, all sympathy shifted away from the blacks, who had suffered under Smitty's racist regime, and back to the head jocks, who were now just viewed as total innocents trying to defend themselves against superior numbers. I started thinking how could *The Tin Whistle* help end all this senseless violence?

Meanwhile, Charlie Geron, a columnist in *The Tin Whistle* was stoking the flames, challenging any jock in school to a one-on-one match, and I'm sure Charlie would have gladly taken anyone on, had anyone ever accepted. Jim Cole, former lead singer of the Finchley Boys, came back to school for a few days while still living at Eric Swenson's house. One morning Cole was asked to read the day's announcements over the public address system and he read them all perfectly, except for the fact he added one additional of his own: "the AFS [Association for Foreign Students] will be sponsoring a race riot in the cafeteria at noon. Bring your own weapons." You see, the previous day, a racial altercation had cleared the lunchroom momentarily, and everyone was still on edge from that incident. But Cole sure let the air out of the balloon with that fake announcement. We all laughed heartily together, blacks, white, jocks. Cole, meanwhile, bounded straight out of the school and never came back. I guess the Grandmaster of Mayhem had been searching for a proper exit line and that was it. So this was the background to the student elections taking place at Urbana High in the fall of 1968.

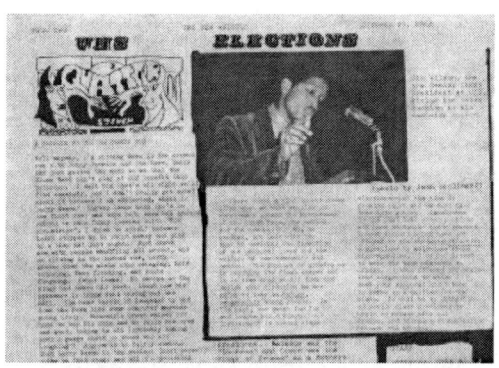

Jim Wilson's speech for class president reprinted in the Tin Whistle.

My hat must have provided the final magic touch, because Larry certainly wowed the crowd that afternoon. It may have been his first "great performance," although certainly not nearly his last. Sauntering across the stage in a sort of Fred-Astaire-meets-Lenny-Bruce persona, Larry launched into a beatnik poem by Shel Silverstein lifted out of *Playboy* magazine. (I wonder if any students thought he was jivin' off the top of his head?) When this performance was over, Larry asked everyone to vote for Jim Wilson. And then Jim took the stage and gave a very serious speech about the need to address the racial communication issues at the school, a speech that soon swept Jim into office, with all of us in full support.

Except for that slight last-second, ego-meltdown by Larry, who, after his grand performance was over, was swarmed by sycophants urging him to stay in the race. I remember Larry coming up to me soon after he heard I was urging people to vote for Jim Wilson. He was super mad and saying "I am running!" I was crestfallen at that moment because I knew Larry was letting the magic slip away. It was a sort of Frodo-won't-let-go-of-the-ring moment.

179

You might wonder, why the hat at the last minute like that? Larry was still under haircut rules at the time, and I had just recently escaped them. I think I wore that hat so much because it helped disguise the fact my hair was really shorter than it should have been. And I think that's the same reason Larry employed it, as his character that day was an ultra hipster. And Larry was running against another white dude with almost shoulder-length blonde hair. So the hat may have been the perfect touch to his act. You'll also notice that in my column for that month, I'd created these white and black devils as a comic illustration, representing, no doubt the twin paths that had emerged at the beginning of the counterculture, one of which involved violence and one of which did not.

Jim Wilson was now the first black senior class president in Urbana High history, thanks in no small part to Larry Green throwing him his support (and then taking it back too late for anyone to notice), and the fact no member of the U-Club ran against him, and as a result of the football coach unfairly blackballing him off the team. And the first thing Jim did was ask every student to fill-out a one-page query on racial attitudes. We didn't know it at the time, but Jim edited these responses and was going to have them read aloud in public assembly, just to show us how crazy deep our collective racism really ran. See, most of us were living in our own little worlds. Some of the more liberal families certainly had no idea of the savage beliefs being held by some of their fundamentalist fellow students. The reading of selected passages of these forms caused great stress, as evident in a photo of the reaction published in the yearbook .

Charlie Geron, in fact, rushed the backstage and began pounding on the door, eventually reduced almost to tears. Charlie wanted to beat-up the students reading those ugly responses behind a screen. Charlie didn't realize those weren't the same students who thought black people smelled bad and were spawns of the devil, that was just Albie Fisher and some friends of Jim's.

The school reacts in shock to Jim's program.

Jim's student forum on racism worked to perfection, however, as no one in the school from that day forward ever asserted there was no such thing as racism at Urbana High. The only question now was, what was Jim going to do to try and get rid of it?

MacBird!

After JFK was assassinated, the country went into deep shock. Very few people wanted to dwell on the event, or even consider evidence of CIA involvement. In fact, the mood of the country was similar to the post 9/11 environment, which left many people unable and unwilling to consider alternative conspiracy theories other than Osama bin Laden did it.

In any major crime, however, the key is to examine who benefited, and nobody benefited more from the JFK assassination than Lyndon Baines Johnson, an intensely corrupt politician who knew about the event in advance, although he certainly lacked sufficient power to pull it off on his own. In fact, had JFK not been assassinated, Johnson would likely have been jailed due to an ongoing investigation into bribes he'd accepted, a story that wouldn't fully surface until after his death.

Barbara Garson was a leader in the Berkeley Free Speech Movement. In August of 1965, she was speaking at an anti-war rally in Berkeley, when she called the new First Lady: "Lady MacBird Johnson." This slip-of-the-tongue inspired Garson to write a Shakespearean parody based around the Kennedy assassination and the first staged reading of this masterpiece of counterculture literature actually occurred at the Channing-Murray Foundation run by the Unitarian Church in Urbana, Illinois, an event that cemented that church as the beachhead for the blossoming anti-war movement in central Illinois.

The lead character of MacBird was played by none other than my cohort at the time, Brian Ravlin, who I'd first met when he appeared in *A Midsummer Night's Dream* at Urbana Junior High with my brother, Paul. Brian had dropped out of high school and gone to San Francisco in search of Bugsy's brother Don. When he reappeared in Urbana a year later, he seemed an entirely new person. A few days before the show opened, Brian dropped by the high school to visit me and a cheerleader girl squirted him in the face with a squirt gun as a joke. Brian had a huge Afro-like haircut and immense, shaggy sideburns at the time (see picture below). In fact, he was probably the most wildly-flamboyant counterculture character in Champaign-Urbana at the time, although Carl Ellis (Old Carlo) would soon surpass Brian in that regard. Anyway, Brian laughed and gave that girl a little spank on her rear with a spiral notebook he was holding, either his latest poetry or notes for his script. Smitty's son might have been the girl's boyfriend, they certainly ran with the same crowd, for when he saw Brian slap her butt, he just reared back and blindsided Brian with a sucker punch to the face that knocked Brian off his feet and landed him flat on his back. The teacher quickly rushed Smitty's son into the classroom and started class as if nothing had happened. I don't remember much of what followed, other than I went into a slow-boiling rage because nothing was being done since Smitty (the football coach) was the most powerful figure in school. Brian went home and his mom took him to the hospital to get him checked out.

Like most people at the time, I was also having trouble thinking about CIA involvement in the Kennedy assassination. A few others around me were already deep into the citizen research movement (which is the real reason we know the truth today; the government has done nothing but cover-up the trails). But I was stunned by this staged reading, and immediately accepted the transparent truth that life is a giant wheel and the same stories go round and round. Suddenly it was clear the Macbeth tragedy was obviously being played out with new characters in our own time. After watching the show, it became difficult not to become a citizen researcher and I started reading everything I could find on the assassination.

Brian Ravlin (left)

And who do you think played the character of Ken O'Dunc? Why, none other than Eric Swenson, founder of the Finchley Boys, who helped spark the local garage rock movement and then had drifted into acting. In fact, Eric was probably the best actor in the production and was playing the Kennedy role because he could do a perfect JFK imitation, Boston accent and all. Eric had always worshiped Kennedy and no one was more depressed about the assassination than he. Eric even had a portrait of JFK on the wall in his house. I'd already started my own underground newspaper after getting kicked out of the Knight Riders for taking LSD (only a few months later, my former band members turned into huge pot-heads and acid freaks...they even offered to let me back into the band, but I'd already moved on).

I recently went back to take a look at MacBird and rediscovered its brilliance. I think it'd be a popular play today if not for the ending: Bobby Kennedy avenges his brother's death. In the script, Ted Kennedy appears with a cast on his arm and Garson makes it clear the Kennedy's believe Johnson is trying to have them killed as well. Little did we know Bobby would go down within a few years.

For the most part, the script is written in Shakespearean couplets and many of the longer speeches are modern adaptations of Shakespeare's most famous soliloquies. The characters dress in modern suits, except for a colorful plume in their fedoras and tiny toy swords affixed to their waists. Eventually, MacBird became a huge hit on Broadway, launching the career of Stacy Keach.

I wish Garson would revisit this project and update the script with the latest revelations. Certainly the trio of James Angleton, Bill Harvey and Johnny Roselli would make a wonderful addition as primary instigators and eventual assassins. The trio should be forced to keep killing more and more people, and eventually even Roselli, to keep a lid on the conspiracy.

Allen Dulles and J Edgar Hoover would be the masters of the coverup. Kennedy's conflict with the Texas oil cowboys as well as the Eastern Federal Reserve need to be spelled out. And, of course, Johnson must voluntarily give up the throne (and then watch Bobby Kennedy get killed by a Dulles-Angleton goon anyway). In the end, MacBird goes back to the ranch in a deep depression and dies relatively young while tremendously unhappy.

Our local production of MacBird was a transforming event in central Illinois and one I still think about. We already had John Cage producing his greatest happenings in our town, I was running the biggest counterculture publication in downstate Illinois at the age of 17, and the Finchley Boys were rapidly becoming one of the most famous garage bands in the State. But we also had some leaders on the other side of the fence, including the mysterious Professor Revilo P. Oliver, whose name spells the same both ways, and who was the leading pundit of the John Birch Society at the time, the first person to announce a conspiracy cover-up in the JFK assassination within days of the event, and a person who probably should have been fired from the University for anti-Jewish rantings, but never was. In Revilo's worldview, the Jews were behind the Communists, who were behind everything else, including the shadow government. Today,

I view the John Birch Society as an intelligence operation, not a legitimate citizen's group, just based on their controversial history and heavy involvement in obvious disinfo. Revilo would eventually split from the Birch Society and join the violent White Power movement, undoubtedly another intelligence op. In another weird twist, Johnny Roselli, one of JFK's assassins, was passing through town frequently at the time to visit his lover, owner of the *Champaign-Urbana News Gazette*, a newspaper I worked for on week-ends to make pocket money.

I just wish Garson (or someone else) would come up with a play like MacBird only about 9/11 because we sure need something to break down the walls of resistance to truth that have been erected to protect the guilty.

Master of Ceremonies

A typical Tin Whistle *layout included text, photos, illos and poetry in a wide variety of styles.*

It wasn't long after I created my underground newspaper *The Tin Whistle* in 1968, that I decided to become a rock concert promoter to raise money and publicity for the paper, which had become an instant success by selling out at four high schools in Central Illinois, even though it was banned at all of them, except Uni High, our local prep school for the best and brightest.

For my first concert, I asked Blues Weed to perform and they agreed. Donny Perrino, the leader and keyboard player, had been my predecessor on bass guitar in the Knight Riders. I couldn't understand why the Knight Riders wanted to get rid of Donny since he was the best musician in the group, however it didn't take him long to start a new band using a couple of the best high school age blues musicians in town. Unfortunately, a few days before the concert, Blues Weed pulled out, leaving me scrambling to find a substitute band. Naturally, I wanted a Friday or Saturday night at a major venue on campus, but that turned out to be difficult and expensive. I discovered a hall I could rent on Sunday afternoon for cheap, although I didn't realize how difficult it would be to get people to a concert on a Sunday afternoon. At the last minute I got my former band, the Knight Riders, to agree to perform for around $100. The total budget on the event was probably around $200 and admission was $5, so I only needed 40 paid attendees to break even, and the hall easily held over 300. I set up 40 folding chairs in front of the stage and left the back of the hall open for dancing.

For some reason, I decided to drop acid shortly after the doors opened. This was not a good idea because as soon as I started coming off, some of my friends started playing mind games and decided to haul me down to the front of the stage and feed me to the speakers while the band was playing. I suddenly got real nervous about the cash in the moneybox, and inexplicably decided to leave the concert with the money in order to put it in a safe place. About four of my friends came with me, and we stopped by Chug Wyatt's house so I could drop something off. My friends pretended to drive off without me as soon as I got out of the car. I could see them waving money from the cash box out the car windows as they drove off laughing and celebrating. Fortunately, they just circled the block and then picked me up and took me to my parent's house, where I dropped off the cash box with my mom.

When we got back to the concert, the show was just ending, and the band wanted to get paid instantly. They said they needed cash because they'd borrowed the amps for the show from another band and needed to put $10 on each amp when they returned them. And they got one of the toughest black kids in town to intimidate me and make sure they got paid right then.

I was tripping pretty heavy while this beefy black dude was threatening to beat the shit out of me unless I produced the money for the band instantly. I ended up calling the foreign student who had bankrolled the first issue of the *The Tin Whistle*. He gave the band some money, which allowed me to leave with my face intact. But the incident really burned whatever bridges I had with my former band, and I never really spoke to any of those guys again.

Meanwhile Donny Perino turned into a hermit, possibly due to his addiction to marijuana at an early age. Far as I know, he still lives in Urbana, but no one has seen him in decades. I hope he's ok.

My favorite Anti-War Protest

The Illini Union was my home away from home during the 1960s. The original building had recently been renovated and greatly expanded, although my favorite hangout remained The Tavern, located in the basement of the original building. The Tavern had a sort of bohemian coffeeshop feel to it and was a magnet for counterculture types like me. I spent most of my time in those days navigating between Turk's Head, House of Chin, Union Tavern and Red Herring, all of which were within a block or two of each other.

I loved hanging out at the Union bookstore because they let students sit in chairs and read any book without buying it! I'd spend hours in there reading paperback novels. One of my favorite moments came when I walked out and just happened to bump into Carl Ellis and Timothy Leary, who had just crossed paths for the first time and instantly recognized themselves as long-lost comrades-in-arms. I think it began with Carl making some Oriental display of respect and offering his hand, but it ended with both of them embraced in a bear hug. Leary was in town to give a speech later that day in one of the Union ballrooms.

After the Vietnam draft heated up, several anti-war organizations sprouted on campus and draft card burnings became a regular event on the south deck of the Union. Eventually, this deck became officially known as the "free speech area," and impromptu rallies began happening there that alternated between folk songs and speeches against the war. At this time, however, most people in the community still supported the war and a local fraternity responded to these anti-war efforts by holding a blood drive for soldiers overseas.

My favorite anti-war event happened when a big muckity-muck of the draft came to one of the ballrooms to deliver a speech on how the new lottery system was going to work. But after he'd been speaking for only a few seconds, a cue was given and a couple dozen people, including me, put on black hoods with skull faces and stood up on our chairs. Meanwhile, the double doors flung open and a casket paraded into the room. As the casket wound around the room, the black skulls lined up behind it in a silent death march. We ended up marching out of the ballroom pretty quick and planned to exit the building in an orderly fashion and go to the Turk's Head. But as we left the ballroom, we saw campus police rushing towards us, so we quickly veered into a nearby elevator and pushed the "up" button.

Knowing the cops could see which floor we were headed for, we exited the elevator and ran down a long hallway to a different set of elevators, got inside and pushed the "down" button, returning to our original floor. Meanwhile, cops were running all over the building, trying to locate the casket while we stayed one floor and one step ahead of them, laughing all the way. It was a scene right out of the Keystone Kops.

Finally, the cops did corner the casket, and a kid from Uni High who was a year younger than me jumped on top and began delivering a passionate anti-war speech. He was standing under a portrait of Red Grange, the galloping ghost himself, and I remember thinking, "I wonder what Red might think of us now?"

I never see any references to this protest online, although it was my favorite action of all the ones I participated in. Later, there'd be a brief riot in the Union after the school tried to do something about the fact that out of 30,000 students at the U of I in 1967, less than 300 of them were black. After the assassination of Martin Luther King, Jr., statistics like that were especially revealing of the institutionalized racism that afflicted the state. So the U of I hastily set up a program designed to bring 500 black students into the school for the fall semester in 1968. Unfortunately, many of them quickly decided they were being treated like second-class students and demanded to see Chancellor Jack Peltason immediately, not in his office, but in the Union Art Gallery, where hundreds of them had assembled for a sit-in. Peltason was told the situation was too unruly for such a meeting so he decided to close the building instead. That's when a few of the students began slashing paintings. I wonder today who those slashers were and what the point of attacking that artwork might have been? Today, that sort of activity seems more like the work of an FBI dirty tricks informant.

190

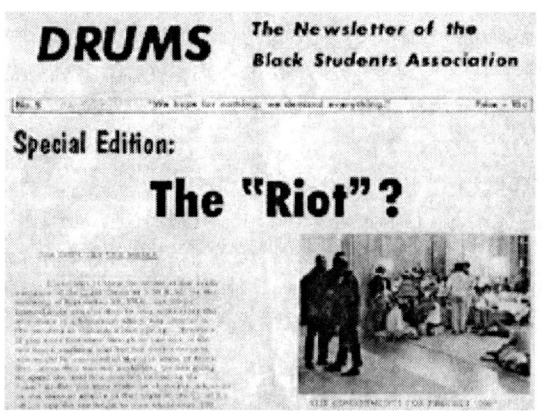

Newsletter of the University of Illinois Black Student's Association.

We knew the FBI was sending dirty tricks specialists to infiltrate our anti-war scene, as they could often be quickly identified as the guy demanding some crazy violent action, like trampling the Morrow Plots, the country's oldest continuous agricultural research center, as if the Morrow Plots had something to do with the War in Vietnam? Despite knowing the FBI was orchestrating the violence, we were helpless to stem the tide, as radical actions got increasingly violent, finally erupting in full-scale riots in 1970.

It was strange for me to see these people getting hostile with Jack Peltason. To me, Jack was just a nice guy, a good friend of my family and the father of my brother's best friend. Many of us had grown up together in Stadium Terrace, a low-cost housing development built as barracks during the war on the west side of the football stadium and later transformed into cheap housing for married graduate students. In the early 1950s, polio swept through the community, and Bugsy's dad was one of the unfortunates who contracted that terrible disease. Many of the families that went through Stadium Terrace remained close long after the barracks were torn down.

191

After I graduated with a degree in playwriting, I sent an application to Yale Drama Graduate school, including a copy of my play that had been performed at the National College Theater Festival. Jack Peltason wrote a letter of recommendation for me. I remember going to his office for the first time to ask him for the letter. He was really shocked to hear I was applying to Yale. "Isn't that the very heart of the establishment?" he asked me with a wink, well aware of my radical activities. As could have been predicted, however, Yale didn't want me, so I took a year off to travel in Europe and then applied to get a Masters in Science in Journalism from the U of I.

Born Again Hippies

It takes more than a bag of weed to forge a hippie heart. In fact, most of the time, it takes a major ceremony. I spent a long time searching for answers throughout much of the sixties, but I didn't get truly "zapped" until I attended the Woodstock Music & Arts Festival in the summer of 1969.

I'd planned to meet up with Larry Green and Carole, but they were coming from New York City, while I was traveling south from Cape Cod. Once the highway was closed, I feared they'd been turned away.

As it turned out, however, meeting people at Woodstock was no problem. I ran into James "Chef Ra" Wilson almost immediately. I could tell Jim was already zapped. His life would never be the same. Davy Goldwasser, one of the brightest kids in town, stumbled into our camp in the middle of the sea of humanity. When the rain came, we hid under a tarp Davy had brought along. A photo of us appeared in a German magazine. Note the fence I constructed to keep people off my comfy bed. I remember Larry was really pissed at me for changing into my dry clothes right after the rain blew over. I think it was about the only negative second we experienced at the event, and Larry was afraid the straw we were sleeping on was getting muddied, although I suspect the real reason was Carole's frequent whispering in my ear.

The author, Carole, Larry and Davy keeping dry at Woodstock.

The zapping I got at Woodstock sure faded over the years, as I went back to college in California and then back to Illinois as I had to work my way through a couple of degrees. I'd lost most of that non-violent telepathic energy by the time I hit *High Times* in the late 1980s. When I'd first moved to New York at the beginning of the 1980s, my primary interest had been experimental theater, and Julian Beck's Living Theater was one of my biggest influences. Imagine my surprise when I saw Julian standing on the corner outside my apartment on 98th Street shortly after moving in.

Many years later, however, I'd meet Julian's son, Garrick Beck, one of elders of the Rainbow Family of Living Light. Soon after meeting Garrick, I attended my first National Rainbow Gathering, which is where I got re-zapped.

That's when I also decided to inject some ceremonial elements into the Cannabis Cup and WHEE! festivals I'd created. I was hoping to pass this non-violent culture on down and let the future generations get zapped by our peace-love vibrations. We really need a return of this culture in order to heal some of the trauma of the last few years, especially all the shootings. By showing respect for non-violence, you can help turn the children away from the allure of violence. But when you disrespect the cultures of non-violence, you actually urge children toward prejudice and bigotry.

Sad to say, many people walked through these ceremonies over the years and never got zapped by anything. Nothing even close. If anything, they developed a further hatred for hippies, vegetarians and the Rainbow Family. However, there were plenty of born-again hippies created as well. I know because many of them came up to me and told me so, while thanking me effusively for putting them back on the path of non-violence.

The Chain Whipping Incident

Did you know the world's only hippie memorial is located along the Illinois Central train tracks in Arcola, Illinois? The town I grew up in was actually a hotbed of radical activity in the 1960s. The fledgling Students for Democratic Society (SDS) picked Urbana, Illinois, in fact, as the site for their 1965 conference, and hundreds of members arrived from all around the country. Soon, we had the state's best garage band, The Finchley Boys, as well as the country's greatest experimental artist, John Cage, both performing in our little community 120 miles south of Chicago. We also had the first landmark performance of a masterpiece called "MacBird!" which theorized JFK had been murdered and President Johnson was an accomplice in the crime.

Jim "Chef Ra" Wilson was my high school senior class president, the first black elected to that position. He organized the first black appreciation celebration in the history of Urbana High. It was held late at night and included free soul food and a series of performances by notable black musicians who were also students at the school.

My best friend Larry, recently arrived from Baltimore, somehow became one of the star attractions of the evening by commanding a gaggle of black girls around him at all times, all constantly cracking up at his improv performances. The alpha chick among them was also the girlfriend of the star of the show, who played keyboards and sang, among many other talents. I remember him from the stage suddenly stopping the show to ask his girl what she was doing with her arm around Larry Green's neck? Somehow, Larry turned that all around into a big belly laugh and the performance went on. I don't know if any long-term inter-racial relationships were born that night, but it certainly was a wonderfully healing ceremony for all who attended and I hope we left many of our fellow black students with a sense of our appreciation for their culture, despite the institutionalized racism that had afflicted the school up until then and the fact few of us would actually try the chitlins.

Jim's ceremonies would continue to evolve and mature as he grew up. One of his best was his annual appearance in the July 4th parade, which wound its way through much of the town before culminating at the football stadium, where the state's largest fireworks display would be set off come darkness. Jim could often be found in some wild, colorful outfit, roller-skating through the entire parade route and doing circles and stunts the whole way. He was well over 6 foot tall, and had placed third in the state high jump his senior year so his athletic abilities were unparalleled.

In 1968, someone applied for a permit for anti-Vietnam war demonstrators to march in the annual parade and the permit was duly granted on grounds of free speech after a brief court battle even though members of the town councils wanted it denied as un-American and inappropriate. We happened to be driving past Green Street when the protestors were attacked by a gang of men wearing hard-hats, some of whom wielded clubs and chains. Jim Cole, leader of the Finchley Boys, was one of the protestors and would later describe grabbing a fist aimed at his face and then realizing it belonged to someone he knew quite well. I really felt I'd missed out on something exciting, but I wasn't much of a street fighter anyway. My time, however, was soon coming.

Later that day, I was hitchhiking with Larry and Carole. Carole, at this point, had become Larry's girl friend. I'd already read *The Sun Also Rises* so the part of discarded ex-lover who hangs on for dear life had already been portrayed as a noble cause. Whenever I saw films like *Butch Cassady and the Sundance Kid*, I immediately recognized my role.

Anyway, a white car slowed to a stop. "We'll take the girl, but we won't take you," said a dude in the backseat, whose mouth seemed full of marbles. He had a southern, redneck accent and was barely understandable. I looked inside the car and noticed some guys in uniform and thought I saw a hardhat on one of the seats.

"Would you like to ride with these guys?" I asked Carole, who, of course, said, "No."

As I was explaining the situation, the dude in the shotgun seat reached down on the floor and produced a steel chain. He opened the car door and I began backing away from the car, while holding Larry and Carole behind me. But we couldn't back up fast enough for the dude swung that four-foot chain and it whipped around my side while he began yelling about his contempt for longhaired hippies like me. At this point, my only thought was to get Carole out of there before the other three dudes got out of the car and

196

tried to abduct her. She seemed to be the real center of interest in all situations, so I grabbed her arm and yelled, "Run!"

Meanwhile, Larry stepped around me and confronted this dude. Larry had the supreme confidence he could talk his way out of any situation as well as being somewhat fearless. Larry probably began with some comment like: "Hey, now wait a minute, this doesn't call for violence..." Meanwhile I was already halfway around the house wondering why Larry hadn't taken off running with us when I yelled "Run!." Although I couldn't see what was happening, I soon surmised that Larry had been pushed into a large bush and beaten on his back a couple times with the chain.

Some guardian angel appeared out of nowhere, claiming to be a Vietnam War Vet. The dude beating on Larry was talking about the war while he was beating on him. And this Vet wanted him to know that all Vets didn't feel like him and that he should leave Larry alone and let him go. Carole, meanwhile, refused to stay hidden on the other side of the house with me since she was delirious with concern over Larry.

Eventually the three of us reunited and the car drove off. Back at her house, Carole scolded me pretty harshly for running away from the scene and abandoning Larry like that after he tried to stick up for me. But we got over it pretty quick and headed back to Campus-town, where everyone was hanging out in front of Turk's Head. Larry showed off his chain marks for all to see while we recounted the story of our adventures. Much later than night, while I was alone in the bathroom, I would finally notice the chain welts across my own back.

Pagan Ceremonies

When I was growing up in the 1960s, the favorite place to go tripping was Allerton Park in Monticello, Illinois. Situated on

197

1,500 acres, this estate was built by an heir to Samuel Allerton's Chicago stockyard fortune named Robert Allerton, who was an avid art collector and one of the leaders of the gay party scene in Chicago. Robert eventually adopted his young gay lover to live with him.

The estate was built in the middle of nowhere, nestled between a stream and reflection pond. The photo I took one afternoon (above) is taken from the South, the stream lies to the right and one could see and hear it from the huge brick deck that juts out from the eastern wing of the mansion. Robert wanted total privacy for his infamous parties, which often lasted for days. He had a private train track built that connected to the Illinois Central line so that his guests could easily travel from Chicago straight to his mansion, which was surrounded by the most beautiful gardens in the state. The track ended a mile from the house, probably because Robert wanted to bring them the final way via open-air, horse-drawn carriages so they could fully appreciate the magnificent landscaping as they entered the estate grounds.

The Sun Singer

These gardens were filled with the most amazing sculptures, the largest of which was titled "The Sun Singer." This bronze statue

198

of Apollo was placed on a huge round pedestal and was the largest of the art works Allerton imported from Europe. The original had been placed in Stockholm harbor and when Robert saw it, he asked the sculptor, Carl Milles, to make a version for him.

Parties went on constantly at the mansion and the guests would usually be asked to change into a costume upon arrival depending on the theme of the week. Robert kept many costume options available for his guests, but some of the most elaborate were Chinese silk robes. I sometimes used to wonder if they had any black robes for some "darker" ceremonies. Apparently, the guests would gather round the Sun Singer in the pre-dawn darkness and then hold a pagan sunrise ceremony. I used to suspect Robert may have been part of some illuminati cult, but later learned that he was probably just a gay party dude, who moved to Hawai'i permanently after his favorite gay bars were closed in Chicago. The end of the Roaring Twenties had brought a close to Robert's revelry in Illinois. That plus the Depression, which made it far too expensive to maintain a 1,500 acre estate.

Allerton Foo Dog

The garden closest to the mansion contained 22 beautiful Foo Dogs from China, although today most of these have been sadly vandalized. Near the Foo Dog garden was a pagoda with a giant gold Buddha inside, probably the largest in the state if not the

199

country. This was a wonderful place to trip because not only could you enjoy miles of hiking through wilderness trails, but you'd constantly be stumbling into these wonderful gardens filled with plants, flowers, ponds, and fantastic sculptures. To give you an idea, there was a Herb Garden, Walled Garden, Triangle Parterre Garden, Peony Garden, Chinese Maze Garden, Hidden Garden, Sunken Garden. There was also an amazing sculpture hidden in the forest titled "Death of the Last Centaur," a tribute to the demise of paganism. Most of the gardens were designed to be ceremonial sites and one wonders about the nature of some of these gay ceremonies and whether any orgies were involved. One thing for sure, Robert put a wall with guard dogs around the property closest to the road. He was very serious about maintaining his privacy.

The Allerton mansion.

Paul Tyner, a math prodigy grad student at the University of Illinois, became a local celebrity upon publishing his first novel, *Shoot It* in 1968. The first time I became aware of Paul, he appeared at a huge acid party at Allerton driving a VW bug. The car was small enough to fit between the concrete blocks that had been erected to keep vehicles off the trails and out of the gardens.

Paul was high on LSD, driving that bug full speed straight at the pagoda. I don't remember if he crashed or not, probably he did since he was certainly out-of-control that day and drinking heavily.

The sky was the limit for Paul. His book had been praised in the press by the most respected critics, and a movie deal was struck. The book was brilliant, although it's very hard to find a copy these days. It reminded me somewhat of *A Separate Peace* by John Knowles in that the protagonist commits a crime on impulse and then tries to blot it out of his memory by constructing a wall of denial. Both books are really about the power of the subconscious mind, but Knowles' takes place in an exclusive Ivy League prep school, while Tyner's is set amongst the Chicago working-class.

Unfortunately, Paul slid into alcoholism pretty quick and went from the most celebrated novelist in the state to working as a bus boy at the House of Chin just to get free beer. If anyone has any info on him, I'd appreciate some updates. I'm sure he died young and broke.

Shoot It *by Paul Tyner was a prophetic book on police violence.*

Meanwhile, in 1974, the film adaptation was released under the title: "Shoot It Black, Shoot It Blue," starring Michael Moriarty and Paul Sorvino. Although well reviewed, this film is never shown anywhere it seems. Someday I hope Paul's legacy can be restored.

My 420 Story

In 1990, *High Times* news editor Steve Bloom returned to the office from a trip to the Bay Area and brought with him a flyer to an April 20th event to be held at the top of Mount Tamalpias in Marin County. The flyer indicated that "420″ was California police code for "marijuana smoking in progress." Bloom thought the flyer was funny and a bit ridiculous. I felt otherwise. Since I'd recently started my research into the spiritual history of cannabis use, I immediately seized on the flyer as evidence of the spiritual power of cannabis and began holding "420 or fight" ceremonies at *High Times*. And the next time I returned to produce the annual Cannabis Cup in Amsterdam, I held an open council at 4:20 pm that everyone was invited to. All the early 4:20 councils at the Cannabis Cup were videotaped and segments can be viewed in my history of the Cannabis Cup on Youtube.

Aside from the 4:20 pm council, the Cannabis Cup crew, specifically the Temple Dragons, began holding 4:20 am celebrations at the Quentin Hotel lobby. These soon became very crowded as word leaked out that this was the best party at the Cannabis Cup. Hundreds of people took photos of themselves in the Quentin lobby next to a clock as proof they attended a 4:20 am Cannabis Cup ceremony. During this time, I also began using 420 as a central element of the Whee! festivals that soon appeared in five states.

The 420 events at the Cannabis Cup became so popular, in fact, that the tour agent, Air Tech, decided to change the name of the official tour to the event to "420 Tours." They set up a website under that name and were soon contacted by Steve Waldo, who indicated that he and his friends had started the 420 fad. I flew out to San Francisco to meet with Steve and check out his claims. I returned to the office a few days later and announced I'd discovered the true origins of 420.

Thus began my long odyssey trying to convince the world about the true history of 420. Now many people spread many stories and try to stake claims on having a "better" explanation. But no one can document the use of the term "420″ as a reference to marijuana prior to 1971, other than Steve Waldo.

The New Pot Enlightenment

THE NEW POT ENLIGHTENMENT IS BROUGHT TO YOU BY
THE POT ILLUMINATI

Will cannabis legalization sweep the world with a steady stream of cities, states and countries following the examples set by Washington and Colorado and now Uruguay? I sure hope so. However, with great deams come great responsibilities. What we need now to accompany legalization is a maturing attitude toward cannabis, what I call a New Pot Enlightenment.

Unfortunately, the image of the average stoner is not particularly attractive, and for good reason since stoners are most often portrayed as dumb slacker slobs. But this was not always the case. In the 1930's, vipers were actually dapper cats with refined taste in fashion and a deep understanding of blues and jazz. So what we really need is a path back to this forgotten past, a time when cannabis use was cool and carried zero negative stigma.

Enlightenment doesn't come around often, by the way, and we just had a major wave 50 years ago in the 1960s with the initial breakdown of fundamentalism. Prior to that, great enlightenment eras occurred during the Age of Reason (circa 1650), and the Renaissance (circa 1450), each wave tied to advances in science and technology as well as publishing and the arts.

The New Pot Enlightenment may be an echo boom from the sixties, but I believe it is more because it's riding a new technological leap: the Internet. The Earth is becoming something of a global village and tools for education and enlightenment have never been so easily accessed. Intelligent youth who escape the dominant programming (towards war and violence) can advance in knowledge quickly as long as they can distinguish the few honest websites from the mountains of disinfo.

I was introduced to cannabis while in high school in Central Illinois, and most of it was ditch weed and probably never got us high at all. We'd harvest in the summer, long before any mature buds had formed, and didn't know the difference between males and females. We stripped leaves off the stalks and smoked them. I remember sitting in my kitchen one afternoon babysitting a tray of leaf I was drying out to smoke. I thought my parents were out playing golf, but my dad unexpectedly appeared and dashed into the house, smelled the odor, opened the oven, and said: "what's this?"

Without hesitating I replied: "Oh, that's my leaf collection, I'm drying it out so I can press it into a book." I don't know if he entirely bought this lie, but it was enough to put him back on whatever mission he was on for he closed the oven and went upstairs and was soon gone.

However, the potency of cannabis today is far beyond that ditch weed of the 1960s and may even pose a possible threat to some youth if they become too attracted too early. But before launching into this lecture, I should point out by far the biggest threat to our youth remains chemical pills and the faster we can end the reign of Ritalin and Paxil, the healthier our children will become. Entire generations are being force-fed these synthetic substances and getting off them is incredibly difficult, much worse than kicking cannabis. But at the same time, we must recognize the dangers of cannabis abuse for the young. I see no harm in teens experimenting, but if they develop a daily habit (and don't have a legitimate medical need), it may hold them back.

I don't believe cannabis causes amotivational syndrome, anymore than video games or watching television does, but young people who medicate constantly may settle for less because they're comfortable, which is why cannabis intoxication used to be called the "farmer's vacation." Long vacations are great for people in retirement years, but not so great for students in the midst of capturing their life skills. If I was in college, I'd avoid binge drinking and breakfast bong hits. In fact, you can't really make a strong case for daily cannabis use (without a medical need) for anyone under the age of 21 because it takes that long for brains to fully develop. Obviously, many will experiment long before, and we should not punish but guide them toward responsible use through education and ceremony.

Under what circumstances should parental consent of cannabis use be considered? The introduction of cannabis represents a vital right-of-passage and we are in dire need of ceremonies to help make cannabis more socially acceptable. When a teenager contributes to adult vibrations (cooking, cleaning) and works hard as an adult on adult activities (chopping wood, carrying water), it's time to recognize them as entering adulthood. This comes at different times for different people, but usually appears around age 18, when a sense of maturity begins to manifest. At this point it may be harmful to withhold adult sacraments at major family ceremonies.

In fact, this is the way alcohol is treated and first use often begins with a sip at a holiday family ceremony. It's at such ceremonies adults break off from children for their secret cannabis ceremony, where those who are making the right-of-passage will get high with adult family members for the first time. It's important to use the sacrament sparingly in these rituals. Just as you might allow a sip of wine at New Year's Eve (but not pour a glass of Jack Daniels) great caution should always be the guide when introducing anyone to cannabis. First time users typically experience no effects from cannabis, which is fine, but others can be easily induced into a panic attack. And keep in mind, cannabis is not for everyone, and if one has a bad reaction, they should probably avoid it. First impressions are everything.

My idea of a great cannabis ritual is to have all the adults take a hit off a vaporizer and then start a jam session or an OM circle, although any sort of yoga or sports like volley ball or touch football works as well and can accelerate the harmonization process, which is key function of most family ceremonies.

I was around 35 when I first came to High Times and had never been a daily user of cannabis except for a couple of brief stretches. On the other hand, I'd also never turned down a free hit. I'd seldom bought it though, just relied on friends to provide. Foremost among these was Jimmy "Chef Ra" Wilson, who was the first person I contacted after I got the job at High Times. Jim had been the leading student activist from my high school, heavily influenced by Stokely Carmichel and H. Rap Brown of the Student Non-violent Coordinating Committee (SNCC). I'd helped elect him senior class president at Urbana High School in Illinois. Jim was the star end on our football team, but one day the coach decided not to allow him into another game. Instead he kept Jim on the bench suited up for the rest of the season with nowhere to go.

As a result, Jim never got the expected football scholarship to attend college, but he did end up going to Woodstock immediately after graduation and visited Jamaica soon thereafter. The next time I saw him, he had dreads and was doing a radio show with a touch of Jamaican patois. He'd gone from worshipping Stokely

Carmichael to worshipping Bob Marley and was the greatest emcee and host of my high school era. He spread joy and zest for life wherever he went. I never saw him do or say anything the least bit sketchy as his principles of non-violence and respect for all humans were unwavering.

So when I think about the New Pot Enlightenment, I think about the Great Chef Ra. Cannabis represents the end of bigotry, cultural hatred and war for religion. It's the sacrament of peace. Since our society suffers immensely from an overdose of violence, anything we can do to manifest non-violence is of great value. And that's why a big part of the New Pot Enlightenment is turning away from violence and recognizing cannabis as the true sacrament of peace.

You can't have true enlightenment without an understanding of where you're at, which is why another big part of the New Pot Enlightenment is the study of deep politics, which makes sense because covert drug policy is a crucial part of the puzzle. Intoxicating substances were mostly legal until the British discovered more profit was made with opium after it was made illegal in China. Pretty soon, opium was illegal everywhere.

Jim Wilson enters Urbana High after being made Senior Class President.

211

Some say British intelligence still plays a role in illegal drugs, although it appears the CIA got control of opium after moving the center of production to Afghanistan. There is no easier way to make profits than illegal drugs, which means any intelligence agency can fund black operations through drug distribution, and I'm sure many of them do since all it takes is a diplomatic pouch.

Part of the New Enlightenment is a realization the CIA Executive Action Program run by Bill Harvey and supervised by James Angleton was responsible for assassinating President John F. Kennedy, and another part is realizing the truth about 9/11 has been withheld by the Pentagon, and whatever that truth may entail, those three buildings could not have come down at near free-fall speed without the use of explosives, and the maneuvers of some of the planes defy normal human abilities, just as no one could have fired three bullets so accurately from a cheap Italian rifle so quickly as Lee Oswald was accused of having done.

Educate yourself on deep political events and understand major crimes require major cover-ups. Study those cover-ups. In regards to the JFK assassination I recommend Evidence of Revision; and for 9/11, The New Pearl Harbor, both documentaries around five hours in length and well worth watching.

And finally, the most important aspect of the New Pot Enlightenment is a willingness to learn from the ceremonies and rituals of all cultures without having to submit to any of their dogmas. Just as plants achieve hybrid vigor, so do cultures when ceremonies are allowed to mix freely. I like ceremonies improvisational and prefer to allow the role of High Priest move around as much as possible so that everyone gets an opportunity to wear the big hat. That's another key to the New Pot Enlightenment: everyone has the same access to the Great Spirit, and access is not based on intelligence or special abilities. The true Bible is written in all our hearts, and easy to find there provided we have not been abused. And if we have been abused or suffer from traumatic stress, cannabis can be the best possible medicine for alleviating those symptoms, just another proof of its magical and sacramental powers.

I started my own corruption-free spiritual institution recently: The Pot Illuminati, a non-violent organization devoted to improvisational creativity and non-violent enchantment, inspired in large part by James "Chef Ra" Wilson. After organizing counterculture ceremonies for High Times for 25 years, I learned a lot about ceremonial magic and needed a place to park some wisdom so it can be handed down. I came upon the idea of a secret Masonic-style lodge that accepts all cultures. We pass the big hat around and there is no dogma: do what you want, just don't hurt anyone. I'm stealing the sigils of the evil Illuminati and turning them to sigils for good. I call it the Grand Lodge of the Pot Illuminati.

But part of the New Pot Enlightenment is understanding we can create pot-friendly societies and it's a good idea to organize in groups so we can establish a ceremonial culture that can be passed down. Only this time around, let's make it corruption-free and more democratic than your average religion? And please don't make it all about a bunch of stoner dudes getting high. There are deeper and more meaningful trails to follow. So I encourage everyone to start their own cannabis societies to honor the vast ceremonial powers of cannabis. Just keep in mind the most important thing I learned from 25 years at High Times: The less you do, the higher you get. If you want to treat cannabis with respect, there can be much magic, but if you want to abuse her powers, she can just as easily transform into an expensive habit with no magic at all. It's not about who can take the biggest bong hit, but who can get the most benefit from the least amount.

Manifesto of the Pot Illuminati

Cannabis has been a constant provider of human welfare throughout humanity's long journey. The time has come for the Pot Illuminati to gather and take our place as stewards of Cannabis. We seek to help dissolve the oppressive laws against our sacrament. We also seek to harness the power and energy of Cannabis for the welfare of the world.

We have long celebrated the great gifts this unique plant offers such as medicine, food, fuel, paper, cordage, paints, plastics as well as the sacramental key to higher realms of consciousness (if used wisely and in moderation). We have patiently waited for humanity to awaken from the ignorance caused by forgetfulness and many of our members have suffered great persecution just for their acknowledgement and love for the many blessings Cannabis has bestowed upon us.

But we now stand at the threshold of a Great Cannabis Re-awakening, a Phoenix rebirth of the mighty healing spirit of Cannabis. The Pot Illuminati, as faithful stewards and advocates of Cannabis, claim our right to determine, shape and protect the future of Cannabis from state and corporate domination and exploitation.

The Pot Illuminati Lodge is a non-political entity that embraces all people regardless of race, religion or national origin. We seek to blend all the great religions, many of which have been perverted to manifest war for profit. We also seek to disarm the dark lords who support Prohibition and we will do this by stealing their sigils, their names, their totems, and bending them all to our vibrations of peace and respect for Mother Earth.

Induction into The Pot Illuminati Lodge is by invitation only.

The Pot Illuminati Grand Lodge Rules and Dogma

There is no dogma: Do anything you like, just don't hurt anybody. However that does not mean we do not study and celebrate the poetry and myths of past religions. We do. However, we feel free to merge concepts from all religions because they are rivers flowing into the same sea.

Improvisation is encouraged at all times: always allow inspiration to manifest and trust your instincts.

The main vibration to manifest is love and compassion and empathy and when we share these vibrations, it fills the Temple with a palpable energy that can be used to heal trauma and one can feel the healing energy in the room long after everyone has left.

The second vibration is fun, as much fun as possible, and pranks and jokes are totally fine, provided everyone laughs when it's over, because if anyone cries, you just created a stain on your karma.

When the Pot Illuminati gather for an improvisational ceremony, no anger or evil telepathic desires should manifest in the Temple, and if someone's energy is not correct, an Illuminated Master must rectify the situation quickly, often done by inviting the person to share some Cannabis.

If someone yells, or starts a violent confrontation inside the Temple, it must be cleared immediately, and everyone should vacate while an Illuminated Master solves the situation. Members should not return until the perpetrator(s) have either left the

Temple or been excused by the Illuminated Master, and the room should be blessed with sage and ceremony and members should pray in silence until the proper vibration returns and normal Temple functions can continue.

No member should ever lie, cheat or steal, and if caught doing so, they should be expelled. Such matters involve the entire membership, or whoever shows up for the trial, and the accused can be saved by an Illuminated Master if he believes the facts are in doubt.

A small jar of Cannabis should be placed on the altar in the Temple at all times in case of medical emergencies. Members always know they can come to the Temple should they require medicine. White powders, hard drugs, and alcohol are not permitted in the Temple. Do not bring weapons of violence into the Temple and the penalty for this violation is permanent expulsion.

Members should not speak of our society to anyone other than a prospective new recruit, nor share our secrets or ceremonies with outsiders.

Please never carry more than a legal amount of Cannabis into the Temple. It is your responsibility to help protect the Temple and the members from persecution. We seek to create a refuge from the storm so our members can share the sacrament in peace, but we cannot allow that peace to be shattered because of excessive amounts of cannabis brought into the Temple.

There are three degrees in our society: Novice, Master and Illuminated Master. Any Master can nominate a potential new Novice and invite that person into the Temple. However, this should never be done lightly. If you nominate someone, you must know their entire history and be sure their nature is non-violent and they don't secretly work as informers or undercover agents. Any Illuminated Master can block the entrance of a new member if he suspects that person's heart is not pure. If you have been involved with violence, you cannot be a member unless all the Illuminated Masters think you have changed your ways. Do not apply or seek membership if you have a history of hurting people or have been arrested for violent activities.

Once you are inducted into our society, you will be given a pin to wear, which you can display or hide. However, you should never brag or boast about your membership, nor draw attention to your pin, but if someone asks what that is, feel free to whisper the words: "Pot Illuminati" and then put a finger to your mouth and go "shhhh" and say no more on the subject.

If you have been persecuted and put in jail for Cannabis and have no violence attached, you are allowed skip the Novice degree and move straight to Master status. This is done to heal the great traumas caused by Prohibition and recognize the suffering inflicted on our culture.

This is a work in progress, and you can help my making suggestive comments.

I'm a writer, journalist, filmmaker, event producer and counterculture and cannabis activist, and was born and raised in Urbana, Illinois. I started out writing black comedy, but I'm best known as the first reporter to document hip hop and the instigator of the film *Beat Street*. I also founded the Cannabis Cup, organized the first 420 ceremonies outside of Marin County, while launching the hemp movement with Jack Herer and writing some landmark conspiracy articles. Some of my other books you might enjoy:

**KILLING LINCOLN
THE REAL STORY**
STEVEN HAGER

Why was Lincoln left unguarded when the War Department knew there were serious plots afoot against him? Why was Booth killed when he was locked in a tobacco barn and surrounded by 25 soldiers. Why were two innocents swiftly hanged by a military tribunal and not allowed to even testify in their own defense. You will find the answers in this explosive book.

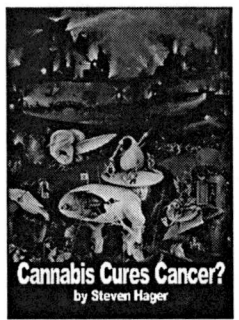

Does cannabis cure cancer? Cancer is a big subject and easily misunderstood. But there is no doubt cannabis has anti-cancer effects, so why does the US government pretend it has no legitimate medical uses?

In the early 1980s, I became the first reporter to travel to the South Bronx to document the origins of hip hop and this book remains the most authentic portrait of the first generation. It was recently updated with never-before-seen photos and illustrations.

CPSIA information can be obtained
at www.ICGtesting.com
Printed in the USA
FFOW02n1322040316
22110FF